CompTIA A+ Exam - Mastery Guide:

The Most Updated Resource to Pass Core 1 and Core 2 Exams at Your First Attempt.

Maxwell Turing

DISCLAIMER

The information contained in this book are for general informational and educational purposes only. This book is not affiliated with or endorsed by the Computing Technology Industry Association (CompTIA), the organization that administers the CompTIA A+ certification exams.

While the authors and publisher have made every effort to ensure the accuracy and completeness of the information contained in this book, we make no guarantee or warranty, express or implied, including but not limited to any warranties of performance, merchantability, or fitness for any particular purpose.

The authors and the publisher shall not be held liable or responsible to any person or entity with respect to any loss or damage caused or alleged to be caused directly or indirectly by the information contained in this book. It should be understood that a certification preparation book like this one is not a guarantee of passing the CompTIA A+ exams.

The strategies and information presented herein represent the views of the authors as of the date of publication. Because of the rate at which the information technology field changes, the authors and publisher reserve the right to update and alter their opinions based on the new conditions.

The ultimate responsibility for achieving exam success lies with the reader.

Table of Contents

Introduction to Computer Systems

A computer system is a complex combination of hardware and software components that work together to perform various tasks and provide valuable services to users. It is a fundamental concept in the field of computer science and information technology. Understanding how computer systems function is crucial for anyone interested in working with computers, whether it be programming, system administration, or general computer usage.

Components of a Computer System:

1. Hardware: The physical components of a computer system are collectively referred to as hardware. This includes the central processing unit (CPU), memory (RAM), storage devices (hard drives, solid-state drives), input devices (keyboard, mouse), output devices (monitor, printer), and various other peripherals that enable the system to perform specific tasks.

2. Software: Software refers to the programs, data, and instructions that tell the computer what to do. There are two main categories of software: system software and application software. System software includes the operating system (OS), which manages the computer's resources and provides a platform for running applications. Application software includes various programs designed for specific tasks, such as word processing, web browsing, and gaming.

3. Operating System (OS): The operating system is the most crucial software component of a computer system. It acts as an intermediary between the hardware and the user, managing resources, scheduling tasks, handling input and output operations, and providing a user-friendly interface. Some popular operating systems include Microsoft Windows, macOS, Linux, and Android.

4. Central Processing Unit (CPU): The CPU is the "brain" of the computer, responsible for executing instructions and performing calculations. It interprets and processes instructions from software and controls the flow of data within the computer system.

5. Memory (RAM): Random Access Memory (RAM) is a volatile memory that temporarily stores data and instructions that the CPU needs to access quickly. It provides fast access to information, allowing the CPU to work efficiently.

6. Storage Devices: Computers use various types of storage devices to store data in a more permanent manner, even when the power is turned off. Common storage devices include hard disk drives (HDDs) and solid-state drives (SSDs).

7. Input and Output Devices: Input devices allow users to provide data and commands to the computer, such as keyboards, mice, and touchscreens. Output devices display or produce the

results of computations, such as monitors and printers.

Computer System Architecture:

The architecture of a computer system refers to the organization and interconnection of its components. The two main types of computer system architectures are:

1. Von Neumann Architecture: This is the classical architecture used in most modern computers. It is named after the mathematician and computer scientist John von Neumann. In this architecture, both data and instructions are stored in the same memory (RAM), and the CPU fetches them from memory one at a time to execute them sequentially. While this architecture is widely used, it can create bottlenecks due to the sequential nature of processing.
2. Harvard Architecture: This architecture separates the memory for data and instructions, providing separate data and instruction buses. This allows simultaneous access to both data and instructions, potentially improving the overall performance of the system. Harvard architecture is often used in specialized systems, such as microcontrollers.

Evolution of Computer Systems:

Computer systems have undergone significant evolution since their inception. They have become more powerful, smaller in size, and widely accessible to people around the world. Some key milestones in the evolution of computer systems include:

1. Mainframes: In the mid-20th century, mainframe computers dominated the computing landscape. These large and expensive machines were used by large organizations and governments for critical tasks such as data processing and scientific calculations.
2. Minicomputers: In the 1960s and 1970s, the development of minicomputers brought computing power to smaller organizations and research institutions. Minicomputers were less expensive and more accessible than mainframes, leading to greater adoption.
3. Microprocessors and Personal Computers (PCs): The invention of the microprocessor in the early 1970s revolutionized computing. Microprocessors allowed the integration of CPU functions on a single chip, enabling the development of personal computers. The introduction of the IBM PC in 1981 marked the beginning of the PC era, making computing accessible to individuals and businesses.
4. Laptops and Mobile Devices: As technology advanced, computers became smaller and more portable. Laptops allowed users to carry their computing power with them, and eventually, smartphones and tablets emerged, revolutionizing the way people interact with computers

2

and the internet.

5. Cloud Computing: Cloud computing is a paradigm shift in how computer resources are accessed and utilized. Instead of relying solely on local hardware, cloud computing allows users to access computing power, storage, and applications over the internet. This has facilitated remote work, collaboration, and the rise of various online services.

6. Internet of Things (IoT): The IoT refers to the network of interconnected devices and objects that can collect and exchange data over the internet. IoT devices, ranging from smart home devices to industrial sensors, have expanded the scope of computing applications.

7. Quantum Computing: Quantum computing is an emerging field that leverages the principles of quantum mechanics to perform computations at an exponentially higher speed than traditional computers. Though still in its early stages, quantum computing holds promise for solving complex problems in areas like cryptography, optimization, and material science.

Challenges and Future Trends:

As computer systems continue to evolve, they face various challenges and opportunities:

1. Security and Privacy: With increased connectivity and reliance on technology, cyber threats have become more sophisticated. Ensuring the security and privacy of data and systems remains a top priority.

2. Artificial Intelligence and Machine Learning: Advancements in AI and machine learning are transforming the way computers process information, learn from data, and make decisions. These technologies are being applied in diverse fields, such as healthcare, finance, and autonomous vehicles.

3. Edge Computing: Edge computing involves processing data closer to the source or the "edge" of the network, reducing latency and bandwidth requirements. It is gaining importance as IoT and real-time applications become more prevalent.

4. Sustainable Computing: The growing energy consumption of data centers and electronic devices has raised concerns about environmental impact. Sustainable computing aims to develop energy-efficient hardware and software solutions.

5. Augmented Reality (AR) and Virtual Reality (VR): AR and VR technologies are transforming the way we interact with computers, offering immersive experiences in various fields, including gaming, education, and training.

1.1 Basic Computing Concepts

Computing is the process of using computers to perform tasks, process data, and solve problems. Understanding some fundamental computing concepts is crucial for anyone interacting with computers, whether for personal use or in professional settings. Here are some key basic computing concepts:

1. Data: Data is raw and unorganized facts or information. It can be numbers, text, images, audio, video, or any other form of digital content. Data is the foundation of all computing processes and is manipulated to generate meaningful information.

2. Information: Information is data that has been processed, organized, and presented in a meaningful way. It provides context and answers specific questions, making it useful for decision-making and understanding.

3. Binary System: Computers represent and process data using a binary system, which uses only two digits: 0 and 1. These digits are the basis of all digital information and are used to represent various forms of data, including text, images, and instructions.

4. Bits and Bytes: A bit is the smallest unit of data in computing and can represent either a 0 or a 1. Eight bits make up a byte, which is the basic unit for representing data in most computer systems. Bytes are used to measure the size of files and storage capacity.

5. Software: Software refers to the programs, applications, and operating systems that control and run on computer hardware. Software allows users to perform specific tasks, such as word processing, web browsing, or playing games.

6. Hardware: Hardware encompasses all the physical components of a computer system, including the central processing unit (CPU), memory (RAM), storage devices, input and output devices, and other peripherals. Hardware is essential for executing software and performing tasks.

7. Algorithm: An algorithm is a step-by-step procedure or set of rules used to solve a specific problem or perform a particular task. It serves as a blueprint for executing tasks efficiently and accurately.

8. Operating System (OS): The operating system is a fundamental software that manages computer resources, provides a platform for running applications, and enables users to interact with the computer. It controls hardware, manages files, and facilitates communication between software and hardware.

9. Graphical User Interface (GUI): A GUI is a user interface that utilizes graphical elements, such

as icons, windows, and menus, to enable users to interact with a computer system more intuitively. GUIs have become standard in modern operating systems and applications.

10. File Management: File management involves organizing and storing data and files on a computer system. It allows users to create, open, save, delete, and organize files and directories.

11. Networking: Networking enables computers to communicate and share resources with each other, whether over a local area network (LAN) or the internet. Networking is essential for data sharing, remote access, and collaboration.

12. Internet: The internet is a global network of interconnected computers and servers that facilitates communication, data exchange, and access to information from anywhere in the world.

13. Cloud Computing: Cloud computing is a model for delivering computing services over the internet. It allows users to access and utilize computing resources such as storage, processing power, and applications from remote data centers. Cloud computing offers benefits like scalability, cost-effectiveness, and accessibility, making it popular for businesses and individuals.

14. Software Development: Software development is the process of creating, testing, and maintaining software applications. It involves several stages, including planning, designing, coding, testing, and deployment. Various programming languages and development methodologies are used to create software to meet specific requirements.

15. Data Storage and Databases: Data storage involves the organization and preservation of data for future use. Databases are specialized software applications used to store, manage, and retrieve structured data efficiently. They play a crucial role in various applications, such as websites, business systems, and data analytics.

16. Cybersecurity: Cybersecurity involves protecting computer systems, networks, and data from unauthorized access, damage, or theft. It includes measures like encryption, firewalls, antivirus software, and user authentication to ensure data and system integrity.

17. Computer Networks: Computer networks are interconnected systems of computers and devices that allow them to communicate and share resources. Networks can be local (LAN) or wide area (WAN), and they enable file sharing, email communication, internet access, and more.

18. Input and Output: Input devices allow users to enter data and commands into a computer system, while output devices present the processed information in a human-readable format.

Common input devices include keyboards, mice, and touchscreens, while monitors and printers are examples of output devices.

19. Software Licensing: Software licensing refers to the legal agreement between the software developer and the user, outlining the terms of use for the software. Different types of licenses, such as open-source, proprietary, and freeware, dictate how the software can be used, shared, and modified.

20. System Updates and Maintenance: Regular updates and maintenance are essential to keep computer systems secure, stable, and functioning optimally. This includes applying operating system updates, security patches, and software upgrades.

21. Troubleshooting: Troubleshooting involves identifying and resolving issues that arise in computer systems, such as software errors, hardware malfunctions, or network connectivity problems. Troubleshooting skills are vital for maintaining and resolving problems in computer systems.

22. Artificial Intelligence (AI): AI is the simulation of human intelligence in computer systems to perform tasks that typically require human intelligence, such as speech recognition, problem-solving, and decision-making.

23. Machine Learning: Machine learning is a subset of AI that involves the use of algorithms to enable computers to learn from data and improve their performance over time without explicit programming.

These are some additional important concepts that complement the fundamental computing concepts mentioned earlier. Together, they provide a comprehensive understanding of how computers and technology impact various aspects of our lives and drive innovation in multiple industries. As technology continues to evolve, these concepts will remain relevant and serve as a foundation for further learning and exploration in the world of computing.

1.2 History of Computer Systems

The history of computer systems is a fascinating journey that spans centuries of innovation and technological advancements. It is marked by the evolution of various computing devices, from simple mechanical calculators to powerful electronic computers and modern-day digital systems. Here are some key milestones in the history of computer systems:

1. Abacus (c. 3000 BC): One of the earliest known computing devices, the abacus, was used for basic arithmetic calculations. It consisted of beads or stones on rods, with different positions representing different place values.

2. Mechanical Calculators (17th-19th century): In the 17th century, inventors like Blaise Pascal and Gottfried Wilhelm Leibniz developed mechanical calculators capable of performing arithmetic operations. These machines used gears, levers, and other mechanical components.

3. Charles Babbage's Analytical Engine (1837): Charles Babbage, considered the "father of computing," designed the Analytical Engine, a mechanical general-purpose computer. Although never built during his lifetime, the Analytical Engine laid the groundwork for modern computer systems with its use of punched cards for input and output.

4. Punched Card Systems (19th-20th century): Punched cards became widely used in the late 19th and early 20th centuries for data input in early computing systems. They were used in machines like the Hollerith Tabulating Machine, which was used for census data processing.

5. Electromechanical Computers (1930s-1940s): Electromechanical computers, such as the Harvard Mark I and the Z3, were among the first programmable computers. These machines used mechanical switches and relays for computation and data storage.

6. ENIAC (1945): ENIAC (Electronic Numerical Integrator and Computer) was one of the earliest electronic general-purpose computers. It used vacuum tubes for computation and was used for scientific and military applications.

7. UNIVAC I (1951): UNIVAC I was the first commercially produced electronic computer. It was used for business data processing and gained fame for accurately predicting the outcome of the 1952 U.S. presidential election.

8. Transistors (1947): The invention of the transistor by John Bardeen, Walter Brattain, and William Shockley revolutionized computer technology. Transistors replaced bulky and unreliable vacuum tubes, leading to the development of smaller, faster, and more reliable computers.

9. Integrated Circuits (1960s): Integrated circuits, also known as microchips, were introduced in the 1960s. These small semiconductor chips contained multiple transistors, enabling further miniaturization and increasing computing power.

10. Microprocessors (1970s): The development of microprocessors, such as the Intel 4004 and 8080, brought computing power to small, affordable devices. Microprocessors laid the foundation for the personal computer revolution.

11. Personal Computers (1980s): The 1980s saw the rise of personal computers (PCs) with user-friendly interfaces, such as the Apple Macintosh and IBM PC. PCs became increasingly popular in homes, businesses, and schools.

12. Graphical User Interface (GUI) (1980s-1990s): GUIs, pioneered by Xerox PARC and popularized

by Apple's Macintosh and Microsoft's Windows operating systems, made computing more accessible and intuitive to non-technical users.

13. Internet and World Wide Web (1990s): The emergence of the internet and the World Wide Web revolutionized communication, information access, and online services, connecting people and computers globally.

14. Mobile Computing (2000s): The proliferation of smartphones and tablets brought computing power and internet access to people on the move, changing the way we interact with technology.

15. Cloud Computing (2000s-2010s): Cloud computing emerged as a paradigm for delivering computing resources and services over the internet, enabling scalable and flexible computing solutions.

16. Artificial Intelligence (AI) and Machine Learning (2010s): AI and machine learning technologies have seen significant advancements, leading to applications in areas like natural language processing, computer vision, and autonomous systems.

17. Internet of Things (IoT) (2010s): The Internet of Things (IoT) is the concept of connecting everyday objects and devices to the internet, enabling them to collect and exchange data. IoT has found applications in smart homes, industrial automation, healthcare, and more.

18. Quantum Computing (2010s): Quantum computing is an emerging field that leverages the principles of quantum mechanics to perform computations exponentially faster than traditional computers. Although still in the experimental stage, quantum computing holds great promise for solving complex problems in various fields.

19. Edge Computing (2010s): Edge computing involves processing data closer to the source or "edge" of the network, reducing latency and improving real-time data processing. Edge computing is particularly important for IoT applications and time-sensitive tasks.

20. Wearable Technology (2010s): Wearable devices, such as smartwatches and fitness trackers, have become popular consumer products, integrating computing power and sensors into everyday accessories.

21. Virtual and Augmented Reality (VR/AR) (2010s): VR and AR technologies have gained traction in gaming, entertainment, education, and training, offering immersive experiences to users.

22. Big Data and Data Analytics (2010s): The proliferation of data from various sources has led to the rise of big data and data analytics. Analyzing vast amounts of data has become essential for businesses and organizations to gain valuable insights and make informed decisions.

23. Autonomous Systems (2010s): Advances in AI and robotics have led to the development of

autonomous systems, such as self-driving cars, drones, and robots, capable of performing tasks without human intervention.

24. Blockchain Technology (2010s): Blockchain technology, popularized by cryptocurrencies like Bitcoin, offers a decentralized and secure way to record transactions and manage digital assets.

25. Quantum Internet (2020s): Quantum internet aims to create a secure and ultra-fast network using quantum communication principles. It has the potential to revolutionize secure communication and data exchange.

The history of computer systems reflects a continuous cycle of innovation, where each advancement builds upon the previous ones, leading to increasingly powerful, efficient, and interconnected computing technologies. As computing systems become more integral to our lives, ongoing research and development will continue to shape the future of technology, driving us towards new frontiers and possibilities. Ethical considerations will also play a crucial role in ensuring that technology benefits humanity positively and responsibly. The journey of computer systems is far from over, and it will undoubtedly continue to shape the world in profound ways in the years to come.

Quiz

1. What does CPU stand for?

   a) Central Processing Unit

   b) Central Power Unit

   c) Computer Processing Unit

   d) Computer Power Unit

2. Which programming language is used to create web pages?

   a) Java

   b) Python

   c) HTML

   d) C++

3. What is the binary representation of the decimal number 15?

   a) 1110

   b) 1011

   c) 1111

   d) 1100

4. Which of the following is a volatile memory?

   a) Hard Disk Drive (HDD)

   b) Solid State Drive (SSD)

   c) Random Access Memory (RAM)

   d) Read-Only Memory (ROM)

5. Which operating system is developed by Apple Inc.?

   a) Windows

   b) macOS

   c) Linux

   d) Android

6. What does GUI stand for?

   a) Graphical User Interface

   b) General User Interface

   c) Global User Interface

   d) General Utility Interface

7. What does the acronym IoT stand for?

   a) Internet of Technology

b) Internet of Things

c) Internet on Things

d) Internet of Computers

8. Which of the following is NOT an input device?

    a) Keyboard

    b) Mouse

    c) Monitor

    d) Webcam

9. Which of the following is a high-level programming language?

    a) Assembly language

    b) C

    c) Machine language

    d) Binary code

10. Which company developed the first microprocessor, the Intel 4004?

    a) Apple Inc.

    b) IBM

    c) Microsoft

    d) Intel Corporation

11. What is the full form of HTML?

    a) HyperText Markup Language

    b) HyperText Machine Language

    c) HyperLink Markup Language

    d) HyperLink Machine Language

12. What does LAN stand for?

    a) Local Access Network

    b) Long Area Network

    c) Local Area Network

    d) Limited Area Network

13. Which type of software allows users to create and edit documents?

    a) Spreadsheet software

    b) Database software

    c) Word processing software

    d) Presentation software

14. What is the process of converting source code into machine code called?

a) Compiling

b) Linking

c) Interpreting

d) Debugging

15. Which component of the computer is responsible for temporarily storing data and instructions?

a) CPU

b) GPU

c) RAM

d) HDD

16. What is the full form of URL?

a) Universal Resource Locator

b) Uniform Resource Locator

c) Universal Remote Locator

d) Uniform Remote Locator

17. Which type of software provides a platform for running applications and managing computer resources?

a) Operating system

b) Application software

c) System software

d) Utility software

18. What does SSD stand for?

a) Solid State Drive

b) Super Speed Disk

c) System Storage Device

d) Secure System Disk

19. Which programming language is commonly used for web development and server-side scripting?

a) JavaScript

b) Java

c) Python

d) C#

20. Which network topology connects each device in a linear sequence?

   a) Star topology

   b) Ring topology

   c) Bus topology

   d) Mesh topology

21. What does the acronym VPN stand for?

   a) Virtual Private Network

   b) Virtual Public Network

   c) Very Private Network

   d) Visible Public Network

22. What does RAM stand for?

   a) Read-Only Memory

   b) Random Access Memory

   c) Rapid Access Memory

   d) Random Area Memory

23. Which programming language is often used for statistical analysis and data visualization?

   a) Java

   b) R

   c) C++

   d) Swift

24. What is the full form of CPU?

   a) Central Power Unit

   b) Central Processing Unit

   c) Computer Processing Unit

   d) Central Programming Unit

25. Which of the following is a non-volatile memory?

   a) RAM

   b) ROM

   c) Cache memory

   d) Virtual memory

26. Which web browser is developed by Google?

   a) Safari

   b) Internet Explorer

c) Firefox

d) Google Chrome

27. Which of the following is an example of a cloud storage service?

a) Microsoft Word

b) Adobe Photoshop

c) Dropbox

d) iTunes

28. Which operating system is open-source and based on the Linux kernel?

a) Windows

b) macOS

c) Linux

d) Android

29. What is the main function of an operating system?

a) Managing hardware resources

b) Running application software

c) Providing internet access

d) Handling user interfaces

30. Which of the following is an example of a secondary storage device?

a) CPU

b) RAM

c) Hard Disk Drive (HDD)

d) Graphics Processing Unit (GPU)

Hardware

Hardware refers to the physical components of a computer system that can be seen, touched, and manipulated. These components work together to process data, execute instructions, and provide a platform for running software applications. Hardware is a crucial part of any computer system, and its capabilities directly influence the overall performance and functionality of the system.

Major categories of hardware components in a computer system include:

1. Central Processing Unit (CPU): The CPU, also known as the processor, is the "brain" of the computer. It carries out instructions and performs calculations to execute software programs. The CPU's speed and number of cores significantly impact the computer's processing power.
2. Memory (RAM): Random Access Memory (RAM) is a volatile memory used to temporarily store data and instructions that the CPU needs to access quickly. RAM's capacity affects the system's ability to multitask and handle large applications efficiently.
3. Storage Devices: Computers use storage devices to store data and software persistently, even when the power is turned off. Common storage devices include Hard Disk Drives (HDDs) and Solid State Drives (SSDs).
4. Motherboard: The motherboard is the main circuit board that connects and provides a platform for various hardware components to communicate with each other. It houses the CPU, RAM slots, storage connectors, and other essential components.
5. Graphics Processing Unit (GPU): The GPU, also known as the graphics card, is responsible for rendering graphics and visuals on the monitor. It is essential for tasks such as gaming, video editing, and graphic-intensive applications.
6. Input Devices: Input devices allow users to interact with the computer system and provide data or commands. Common input devices include keyboards, mice, touchscreens, and scanners.
7. Output Devices: Output devices present information processed by the computer to the user. Common output devices include monitors, printers, and speakers.
8. Networking Devices: Networking hardware enables computers to connect and communicate with each other over a network. This includes network interface cards (NICs), routers, switches, and modems.
9. Power Supply Unit (PSU): The PSU supplies electrical power to the computer's components. It converts AC power from the wall outlet into DC power required by the computer.
10. Cooling Systems: Cooling systems, such as fans and heat sinks, are essential to keep the computer's components from overheating during operation.

11. Peripherals: Peripherals are external devices connected to the computer to extend its capabilities. Examples include external hard drives, webcams, printers, and speakers.

The hardware components in a computer system work together under the control of the operating system to execute software applications, process data, and provide a user-friendly interface. The selection and configuration of hardware are essential considerations for building a computer that meets specific performance and functional requirements.

Let's dive deeper into some of the key hardware components in a computer system:

1. **Central Processing Unit (CPU):**
- The CPU is responsible for executing instructions and performing calculations. It fetches, decodes, and executes instructions from software programs.
- Modern CPUs have multiple cores, allowing them to handle multiple tasks simultaneously, known as multi-core processing.
- CPU clock speed, measured in gigahertz (GHz), determines how many instructions the CPU can execute in a given time frame.

2. **Memory (RAM):**
- Random Access Memory (RAM) provides fast access to data and instructions that the CPU needs to work with.
- RAM is temporary and volatile, meaning its contents are lost when the power is turned off.
- The amount of RAM affects the computer's ability to run multiple programs and handle large datasets efficiently.

3. **Storage Devices:**
- Hard Disk Drives (HDDs) use magnetic storage to store data on spinning disks. They offer larger storage capacities but are relatively slower compared to SSDs.
- Solid State Drives (SSDs) use flash memory and have no moving parts. They are faster, more reliable, and energy-efficient compared to HDDs.
- Other storage devices include optical drives (CD/DVD/Blu-ray), USB flash drives, and memory cards.

4. **Motherboard:**
- The motherboard is the main circuit board of the computer, connecting and interconnecting various hardware components.
- It provides communication pathways for data transfer between the CPU, RAM, storage, and other peripherals.

- The motherboard also contains expansion slots for adding additional hardware, such as graphics cards or sound cards.

5. **Graphics Processing Unit (GPU):**
- The GPU is specialized hardware designed to handle graphics-related tasks, such as rendering images and videos.
- It is critical for gaming, 3D modeling, video editing, and other graphics-intensive applications.
- Some CPUs have integrated graphics, while discrete GPUs are available as separate cards for enhanced performance.

6. **Input Devices:**
- Keyboards and mice are standard input devices that allow users to enter data and commands into the computer.
- Touchscreens, joysticks, game controllers, and scanners are also common input devices.

7. **Output Devices:**
- Monitors display visual information, such as text, images, and videos, generated by the computer.
- Printers produce physical copies of digital documents and images.
- Speakers and headphones provide audio output for sound and multimedia.

8. **Networking Devices:**
- Network Interface Cards (NICs) enable the computer to connect to wired or wireless networks.
- Routers, switches, and modems facilitate data communication between computers and the internet.

9. **Power Supply Unit (PSU):**
- The PSU converts the electrical power from the wall outlet into the appropriate voltage required by the computer's components.

10. **Cooling Systems:**
- Cooling systems prevent the computer from overheating during intensive tasks. They usually consist of fans, heat sinks, and sometimes liquid cooling systems.

Understanding the various hardware components and their functions is essential for selecting, building, and maintaining a computer system that meets specific performance and usage requirements. As technology continues to evolve, hardware components will continue to improve in performance, efficiency, and capabilities, driving advancements in computing and technology as a whole.

2.1 Motherboard, CPU, RAM, and BIOS

Motherboard, CPU, RAM, and BIOS are essential components of a computer system. Together, they form the core foundation of a computer and play crucial roles in its operation. Let's explore each of these components in detail:

1. **Motherboard:**
   - The motherboard is the main printed circuit board (PCB) in a computer system, serving as a central hub that connects and interconnects various hardware components.
   - It provides electrical and data pathways for communication between the CPU, RAM, storage devices, graphics card, and other peripherals.
   - The motherboard contains slots for inserting expansion cards, such as graphics cards, sound cards, and network interface cards.
   - It typically includes ports for connecting external devices, such as USB, HDMI, Ethernet, and audio ports.
   - The choice of motherboard determines the compatibility of other hardware components in the system.

2. **Central Processing Unit (CPU):**
   - The CPU, also known as the processor, is the "brain" of the computer that performs calculations, executes instructions, and controls the overall operation of the system.
   - It fetches and interprets instructions from software programs and processes data accordingly.
   - The CPU's performance is influenced by factors such as clock speed (measured in GHz), the number of cores, cache size, and architecture.
   - Modern CPUs often have multiple cores, allowing them to handle multiple tasks simultaneously through multi-core processing.

3. **Random Access Memory (RAM):**
   - RAM is a type of volatile memory used to temporarily store data and instructions that the CPU needs to access quickly.
   - When a computer is powered on, the operating system and software programs are loaded into RAM, allowing the CPU to work with them efficiently.
   - RAM's capacity and speed directly impact the computer's ability to multitask and handle large applications or data sets.
   - Data stored in RAM is lost when the computer is shut down, which is why it is referred to as volatile memory.

4. Basic Input/Output System (BIOS):

- The BIOS is a firmware program embedded in a chip on the motherboard. It is responsible for initializing the computer hardware during the boot process.
- When the computer is turned on, the BIOS performs a Power-On Self Test (POST) to check if all essential hardware components are working correctly.
- After the POST, the BIOS loads the operating system from the storage device (e.g., HDD or SSD) into RAM, enabling the OS to take control of the computer.
- In modern systems, the BIOS is gradually being replaced by the Unified Extensible Firmware Interface (UEFI), which provides additional features and better compatibility with newer hardware and software.

These four components work together seamlessly to enable the computer to function effectively. The motherboard acts as a platform to connect and integrate all hardware components. The CPU processes instructions and performs calculations, while RAM provides fast access to data for the CPU. The BIOS or UEFI firmware initializes the system and starts the boot process, leading to the loading of the operating system into RAM.

Understanding these fundamental components is essential for building, upgrading, and troubleshooting computer systems, as well as optimizing their performance for various tasks and applications.

5. Expansion Slots and Ports on the Motherboard:

- The motherboard contains various expansion slots that allow users to add additional hardware components to the system. Common expansion slots include PCIe (Peripheral Component Interconnect Express) slots, which are used for graphics cards, sound cards, and other high-speed devices.
- There are also different types of ports on the motherboard that facilitate connectivity with external devices. These include USB ports, HDMI, DisplayPort, audio jacks, Ethernet ports, and more.

6. CPU Socket:

- The CPU socket is a specific slot on the motherboard designed to hold and connect the CPU to the rest of the system. Different CPUs use different socket types, and compatibility between the CPU and motherboard is essential for proper functioning.

7. Dual In-line Memory Modules (DIMMs):

- DIMMs are the memory modules that are inserted into the memory slots on the motherboard.

They come in various capacities (e.g., 4GB, 8GB, 16GB) and speeds (e.g., DDR3, DDR4). The number of DIMM slots on the motherboard determines the maximum amount of RAM the system can support.

8. **Overclocking and BIOS/UEFI Settings:**

- The BIOS/UEFI firmware on the motherboard allows users to access and modify various settings related to system configuration, boot order, and performance.
- Overclocking is a technique used to increase the clock speed of the CPU and RAM to achieve higher performance. It is done through BIOS/UEFI settings, but it requires careful adjustments and may void the warranty if not done properly.

9. **UEFI (Unified Extensible Firmware Interface):**

- UEFI is an advanced replacement for the traditional BIOS. It provides an enhanced graphical interface and offers more extensive pre-boot options compared to the text-based BIOS.
- UEFI supports faster boot times, larger storage capacities, and improved security features, making it the preferred firmware in modern computer systems.

10. **Chipset:**

- The chipset on the motherboard is responsible for controlling and coordinating data flow between various hardware components.
- It includes the Northbridge and Southbridge chips. The Northbridge typically handles high-speed communication between the CPU, RAM, and GPU, while the Southbridge manages lower-speed connections, such as USB, SATA, and Ethernet.

11. **Onboard Graphics (Integrated Graphics):**

- Some motherboards come with onboard graphics capabilities, allowing them to provide basic video output without the need for a separate graphics card.
- Onboard graphics are suitable for everyday computing tasks but may not be sufficient for gaming or graphics-intensive applications.

12. **BIOS/UEFI Update:**

- Manufacturers often release updates for the BIOS/UEFI firmware to fix bugs, improve compatibility, and add new features.
- Updating the BIOS/UEFI should be done with caution, following the manufacturer's instructions, as an improper update can lead to system instability or failure.

Understanding the components and features of the motherboard, CPU, RAM, and BIOS/UEFI is crucial for building a custom computer, upgrading existing systems, and troubleshooting hardware-related issues. As technology advances, these components continue to evolve, delivering enhanced performance, efficiency, and new features to meet the demands of modern computing applications.

2.2 Storage Devices and Power Supplies

Storage Devices:

Storage devices are hardware components used to store data and software persistently, even when the power is turned off. They are crucial for preserving and accessing information in a computer system. There are several types of storage devices, each with its own characteristics and use cases:

13. Hard Disk Drive (HDD):
- HDDs use magnetic storage technology to store data on spinning disks called platters.
- Data is read and written using read/write heads that move over the spinning platters.
- HDDs offer larger storage capacities at a lower cost per gigabyte compared to Solid State Drives (SSDs).
- They are commonly used for storing files, operating systems, and software applications.

14. Solid State Drive (SSD):
- SSDs use flash memory to store data, which is faster and more reliable than magnetic storage used in HDDs.
- SSDs have no moving parts, making them more resistant to shocks and less prone to mechanical failure.
- They offer significantly faster data access times, leading to faster boot times and application loading.
- SSDs are often used as the primary storage drive (boot drive) for operating systems and frequently accessed applications.

15. Hybrid Drives (SSHD):
- Hybrid drives combine the characteristics of both HDDs and SSDs in a single unit.
- They have a small amount of built-in SSD cache to speed up frequently accessed data while still offering the larger storage capacity of an HDD.
- Hybrid drives aim to provide a balance between performance and storage capacity.

16. Optical Drives:
- Optical drives use laser technology to read and write data from optical discs such as CDs, DVDs, and Blu-ray discs.
- While not as commonly used as they once were, optical drives are still useful for installing software and reading optical media.

17. USB Flash Drives:

- USB flash drives are portable storage devices that use flash memory to store data.
- They are convenient for transferring files between computers and often used as a backup or emergency storage option.

18. Memory Cards:

- Memory cards are small, removable storage devices commonly used in digital cameras, smartphones, and other portable devices.

Connectors:

- Power supplies come with various connectors to provide power to different components within the computer system.
- The main power connectors include the 24-pin ATX connector that powers the motherboard and the 4/8-pin CPU connector for the CPU power.
- Additional connectors include SATA power connectors for storage drives, PCIe power connectors for graphics cards, and peripheral connectors for other components.
- Overcurrent Protection (OCP), Overvoltage Protection (OVP), and Short Circuit Protection (SCP):
- Power supplies are equipped with various protection mechanisms to safeguard the components from potential damage.
- Overcurrent Protection (OCP) prevents excessive current from flowing through the power supply's circuits.
- Overvoltage Protection (OVP) guards against voltage spikes that could damage the components.
- Short Circuit Protection (SCP) safeguards the power supply and other components in the event of a short circuit.

19. Fan and Noise:

- Power supplies often have built-in fans to keep the internal components cool.
- The size and quality of the fan impact the overall cooling efficiency and the noise level of the power supply.
- Some power supplies are designed to operate silently, especially in low-power or low-load scenarios.
- Redundant Power Supplies:
- In server environments and critical systems, redundant power supplies are used for increased

reliability.

- Redundant power supplies have multiple units, and if one fails, the others take over to ensure continuous power supply to the system.

It is crucial to choose a power supply that meets the power requirements of the computer system, taking into account the total power consumption of all components, including the CPU, GPU, storage devices, and peripherals. Additionally, considering the efficiency and quality of the power supply helps ensure stable and reliable performance.

Power Supplies:

Power supplies are critical components in a computer system that provide electrical power to all the hardware components. They convert the alternating current (AC) from the wall outlet into the direct current (DC) required by the computer's components. Key features of power supplies include:

1. **Wattage and Efficiency:**
- Power supplies are rated based on their maximum output wattage, which determines how much power they can deliver to the system.
- Higher wattage power supplies are required for systems with high-performance components or multiple GPUs.
- Efficiency is a measure of how effectively the power supply converts AC to DC power. Higher efficiency power supplies waste less energy as heat.

2. **Form Factor:**
- Power supplies come in various form factors, such as ATX, SFX, and TFX, designed to fit different computer case sizes.
- The ATX form factor is the most common for standard desktop computers.

3. **Modular vs. Non-modular:**
- Modular power supplies allow users to connect only the necessary cables, reducing cable clutter inside the computer case.
- Non-modular power supplies have fixed cables, which may lead to extra cables that are not used in the system.

4. **80 PLUS Certification:**
- 80 PLUS certification is a rating system that indicates the power supply's efficiency at various loads.
- Higher 80 PLUS certifications (e.g., 80 PLUS Bronze, Silver, Gold, Platinum) indicate higher efficiency levels.

5. **RAID (Redundant Array of Independent Disks):**
- RAID is a technology that combines multiple storage drives into a single logical unit for improved performance, data redundancy, or both.
- Different RAID configurations, such as RAID 0, RAID 1, RAID 5, and RAID 10, offer varying levels of performance and data protection.

6. **External Hard Drives and Network Attached Storage (NAS):**
- External hard drives are portable storage devices that can be connected to a computer via USB, Thunderbolt, or other interfaces.
- Network Attached Storage (NAS) devices are dedicated storage units connected to a network, allowing multiple users to access and share files over the network.

7. **Data Backup and Data Recovery:**
- Storage devices are essential for data backup and recovery strategies to protect valuable data from loss or accidental deletion.
- Regular backups to external drives, cloud storage, or NAS help safeguard important files and ensure data integrity.

8. **Form Factors:**
- Storage devices come in different form factors, including 2.5-inch and 3.5-inch drives for HDDs and SSDs, and M.2 drives for compact and high-speed storage.

Proper storage device selection ensures efficient data management, fast access times, and reliable data storage. Combining storage devices with backup and RAID solutions helps safeguard data integrity and maintain data availability, especially in critical computing environments.

Overall, understanding the features and specifications of storage devices and power supplies empowers users to make informed decisions when building, upgrading, or maintaining their computer systems. These components are vital for the performance, stability, and reliability of the computer, making careful consideration and appropriate choices essential for an optimal computing experience.

2.3 Peripherals and Expansion

Peripherals:

Peripherals are external devices connected to a computer system that extend its capabilities and allow users to interact with the computer. These devices play a crucial role in enhancing the user experience and enabling various tasks. Some common peripherals include:

1. **Keyboard:**

- The keyboard is an input device that allows users to enter text, numbers, and commands into the computer.
- There are different types of keyboards, including standard QWERTY keyboards, ergonomic keyboards, and gaming keyboards with extra features.

2. **Mouse:**
- The mouse is another input device that allows users to navigate and interact with graphical user interfaces.
- It is commonly used to control the cursor on the computer screen and perform various operations such as clicking, dragging, and scrolling.

3. **Monitor:**
- The monitor is an output device that displays visual information generated by the computer.
- Monitors come in various sizes, resolutions, and panel types (e.g., LCD, LED, OLED) to meet different user preferences and requirements.

4. **Printer:**
- Printers are output devices used to produce physical copies of digital documents and images on paper.
- There are different types of printers, including inkjet printers, laser printers, and all-in-one printers that can print, scan, copy, and sometimes fax.

5. **Scanner:**
- Scanners are input devices that capture images or documents and convert them into digital format for storage or editing.
- Flatbed scanners and document scanners are common types of scanners used in homes and offices.

6. **Webcam:**
- Webcams are video cameras designed for capturing video and audio to enable video conferencing, live streaming, and online communication.

7. **Speakers and Headphones:**
- Speakers and headphones are audio output devices used to listen to sound, music, and multimedia content from the computer.

8. **Microphone:**
- Microphones are audio input devices used for voice recording, video conferencing, and voice recognition.

9. **External Hard Drives and SSDs:**

- External storage devices are peripherals that connect to the computer via USB, Thunderbolt, or other interfaces to provide additional storage capacity.

10. Gaming Controllers:

- Gaming controllers, such as gamepads, joysticks, and steering wheels, provide specialized input for gaming and simulation experiences.
- They are commonly used for gaming on PCs, especially for console-style games.

11. Graphics Tablets:

- Graphics tablets are input devices used by artists, designers, and digital illustrators to create digital art and drawings directly on the tablet's surface.
- They offer pressure sensitivity and precise stylus control, making them popular tools for digital creativity.

12. Touchscreens:

- Touchscreens are displays with built-in touch-sensitive technology that allows users to interact directly with the screen by touching or tapping.
- They are commonly used in smartphones, tablets, all-in-one PCs, and some laptops.

13. Barcode Scanners and POS Devices:

- Barcode scanners are peripherals used in retail and inventory management to scan barcodes for product identification.
- Point-of-Sale (POS) devices are used in retail and hospitality environments for processing transactions.

14. Game Capture Devices:

- Game capture devices allow users to record or stream gameplay from gaming consoles or PCs, making them popular among content creators and streamers.

15. External Graphics Docks:

- External graphics docks or eGPUs are peripherals that enable laptops to connect to desktop-class graphics cards for enhanced gaming and graphics performance.

Expansion:

Expansion refers to the process of adding or upgrading hardware components to enhance the capabilities of a computer system. Expansion options are typically facilitated by the motherboard and its available slots and connectors. Some common expansion options include:

1. Graphics Card:

- Graphics cards are expansion cards that enhance the computer's graphics capabilities for gaming, video editing, and other graphics-intensive tasks.

- They are inserted into PCIe slots on the motherboard and come with their own GPU and dedicated video memory.

2. Sound Card:

- Sound cards are expansion cards that provide improved audio processing and output capabilities compared to onboard audio.
- They can offer features like better sound quality, surround sound support, and multiple audio inputs and outputs.

3. Network Interface Card (NIC):

- Network Interface Cards are expansion cards used to add wired or wireless networking capabilities to the computer.

4. Expansion Cards for Specialized Functions:

- There are various expansion cards available for specialized functions, such as TV tuners, RAID controllers, and USB expansion cards.

5. Additional RAM:

- Adding more RAM to the computer can improve performance, especially when running memory-intensive applications or multitasking.

6. Upgrading Storage:

- Upgrading storage by replacing an HDD with an SSD or adding more storage capacity can significantly improve system responsiveness and data access times.

7. External Peripherals:

- External peripherals, such as external hard drives, printers, and scanners, can be added to the computer to expand its capabilities without opening the case.

8. Additional Displays:

- Additional monitors or displays can be connected to the computer to increase screen real estate and improve multitasking efficiency.

9. Dual Graphics Cards (SLI/CrossFire):

- Some motherboards support multiple graphics cards in a configuration known as SLI (Scalable Link Interface) for NVIDIA GPUs or CrossFire for AMD GPUs.
- Dual graphics card setups can improve gaming performance by combining the power of two GPUs.

10. Additional PCIe Cards:

- Besides graphics cards, there are various other PCIe expansion cards, such as RAID controllers, sound cards, and high-speed networking cards.

11. CPU Upgrades:

- In some cases, it is possible to upgrade the CPU by replacing it with a more powerful model compatible with the motherboard.

12. External Docking Stations:

- External docking stations expand the connectivity of laptops and ultrabooks by adding additional ports such as USB, Ethernet, HDMI, and more.

13. RAM Speed and Capacity Upgrades:

- Upgrading the RAM to higher-speed modules or increasing the capacity can boost system performance, especially for memory-intensive tasks.

14. M.2 and NVMe Drives:

- M.2 and NVMe drives are high-speed storage devices that can be installed directly on the motherboard, providing even faster data access compared to traditional storage drives.

15. Water Cooling Solutions:

- For high-performance systems, water cooling solutions can be used to cool the CPU and graphics card, providing better thermal performance for overclocking.

When considering peripherals and expansion options, it is essential to ensure compatibility with the existing hardware and consider the power requirements and available slots/connectors on the motherboard. For more complex expansion scenarios, such as multiple graphics cards or water cooling setups, adequate power supply capacity and case space are also crucial considerations.

Customizing a computer system with peripherals and expansion options allows users to create a personalized and optimized setup that meets their specific needs, whether for work, gaming, creative endeavors, or other activities.

Quiz

1. What is the primary function of the Central Processing Unit (CPU)?

   A) Display graphics on the monitor

   B) Execute instructions and perform calculations

   C) Store data for long-term use

   D) Provide power to the computer components

2. Which type of memory is volatile and used to store data that the CPU needs to access quickly?

   A) Hard Disk Drive (HDD)

   B) Solid State Drive (SSD)

   C) Random Access Memory (RAM)

   D) Read-Only Memory (ROM)

3. The main circuit board in a computer system that connects and provides a platform for various hardware components is called:

   A) CPU

   B) RAM

   C) Motherboard

   D) Graphics Card

4. Which of the following firmware programs is responsible for initializing the computer hardware during the boot process?

   A) UEFI

   B) BIOS

   C) RAID

   D) SSD

5. What type of storage device uses magnetic storage to store data on spinning disks?

   A) Solid State Drive (SSD)

   B) USB Flash Drive

   C) Hard Disk Drive (HDD)

   D) Optical Drive

6. Which expansion slot on the motherboard is commonly used to insert graphics cards?

   A) PCIe

   B) USB

   C) SATA

   D) VGA

7. What type of device is used to produce physical copies of digital documents and images?

    A) Monitor

    B) Scanner

    C) Printer

    D) Webcam

8. Which peripheral device allows users to interact with the computer by touching the screen?

    A) Keyboard

    B) Mouse

    C) Monitor

    D) Touchscreen

9. What is the purpose of an external graphics dock (eGPU)?

    A) To connect additional monitors to the computer

    B) To enhance gaming and graphics performance on laptops

    C) To provide extra USB ports for peripherals

    D) To increase the storage capacity of the computer

10. Which RAID configuration provides data redundancy by mirroring data across multiple drives?

    A) RAID 0

    B) RAID 1

    C) RAID 5

    D) RAID 10

11. Which type of memory module is inserted into the DIMM slots on the motherboard?

    A) SSD

    B) USB Flash Drive

    C) RAM

    D) HDD

12. What type of connector is commonly used to connect external hard drives and printers to the computer?

    A) HDMI

    B) USB

    C) Ethernet

    D) DisplayPort

13. Which expansion card is used to add wired or wireless networking capabilities to the computer?

A) Sound Card

B) Network Interface Card (NIC)

C) RAID Controller

D) Graphics Card

14. What is the purpose of a UPS (Uninterruptible Power Supply)?

    A) To provide additional cooling to the computer components

    B) To protect the computer from power surges

    C) To convert AC power to DC power for the computer

    D) To provide backup power in case of a power outage

15. Which type of storage device uses flash memory and has no moving parts?

    A) Hard Disk Drive (HDD)

    B) Solid State Drive (SSD)

    C) Optical Drive

    D) USB Flash Drive

16. Which component is responsible for rendering graphics and visuals on the monitor?

    A) Motherboard

    B) CPU

    C) GPU (Graphics Processing Unit)

    D) RAM

17. What does the acronym UEFI stand for?

    A) Unified Extensible Firmware Interface

    B) Universal External File Interface

    C) Unified External Firmware Integration

    D) Universal Extensible File Interface

18. Which type of connector is used to connect the monitor to the computer for displaying visuals?

    A) USB

    B) Ethernet

    C) HDMI

    D) SATA

19. Which peripheral device is used for voice recording, video conferencing, and voice recognition?

    A) Microphone

    B) Webcam

    C) Speakers

D) Mouse

20. Which expansion slot on the motherboard is commonly used to insert sound cards?

    A) PCIe

    B) USB

    C) PCI

    D) RAM

21. What is the purpose of a barcode scanner in retail and inventory management?

    A) To print barcodes on products

    B) To scan barcodes for product identification

    C) To create 3D models of products

    D) To manage product pricing

22. What is the role of RAID (Redundant Array of Independent Disks) in computer systems?

    A) To increase the performance of the CPU

    B) To combine multiple storage drives into a single logical unit

    C) To control the data flow between hardware components

    D) To provide power to the computer components

23. Which type of storage device is commonly used to store data on optical discs such as CDs and DVDs?

    A) SSD

    B) USB Flash Drive

    C) Optical Drive

    D) HDD

24. Which expansion slot on the motherboard is commonly used to insert network interface cards (NICs)?

    A) PCIe

    B) USB

    C) SATA

    D) PCI

25. What is the purpose of an eGPU (external graphics processing unit)?

    A) To provide extra USB ports for peripherals

    B) To increase the storage capacity of the computer

    C) To enhance gaming and graphics performance on laptops

    D) To connect additional monitors to the computer

26. What type of memory is non-volatile and contains the firmware used to boot the computer?

    A) RAM

    B) ROM

    C) SSD

    D) HDD

27. Which expansion card is used to enhance audio processing and output capabilities in a computer system?

    A) Graphics Card

    B) Network Interface Card (NIC)

    C) Sound Card

    D) RAID Controller

28. What is the purpose of a UPS (Uninterruptible Power Supply) in a computer system?

    A) To provide additional cooling to the CPU

    B) To protect the computer from power surges

    C) To convert AC power to DC power for the computer

    D) To provide backup power in case of a power outage

29. What type of connector is commonly used to connect external hard drives and printers to the computer?

    A) HDMI

    B) USB

    C) Ethernet

    D) DisplayPort

30. Which component is responsible for rendering graphics and visuals on the monitor?

    A) Motherboard

    B) CPU

    C) GPU (Graphics Processing Unit)

    D) RAM

Networking

Networking refers to the practice of connecting multiple computers and devices together to share data, resources, and services. It enables communication and data exchange between devices, whether they are located in the same physical location or spread across vast distances. Networking plays a crucial role in modern computing and is fundamental to the functioning of the internet, local area networks (LANs), wide area networks (WANs), and other communication systems.

Key Concepts and Components of Networking:

1. **Network Topologies:**
    - Network topologies define the physical or logical layout of interconnected devices in a network. Common topologies include bus, star, ring, mesh, and hybrid.

2. **Network Protocols:**
    - Network protocols are sets of rules and conventions that govern how data is transmitted, received, and processed in a network. Examples include TCP/IP (Transmission Control Protocol/Internet Protocol), UDP (User Datagram Protocol), HTTP (Hypertext Transfer Protocol), and FTP (File Transfer Protocol).

3. **Local Area Network (LAN):**
    - A LAN is a network that connects devices within a limited geographical area, such as a home, office, or campus. It allows for fast data transfer and resource sharing among connected devices.

4. **Wide Area Network (WAN):**
    - A WAN spans a large geographical area and connects LANs over long distances. The internet is a global example of a WAN, connecting computers and networks worldwide.

5. **Network Devices:**
    - Network devices facilitate communication within a network. Common devices include routers, switches, hubs, network interface cards (NICs), access points, and modems.

6. **IP Addressing:**
    - IP (Internet Protocol) addressing is a system for assigning unique numerical addresses to devices on a network. IPv4 (Internet Protocol version 4) and IPv6 (Internet Protocol version 6) are the most commonly used addressing schemes.

7. **Domain Name System (DNS):**
    - DNS is a system that translates human-readable domain names (e.g., www.example.com) into

IP addresses, allowing users to access websites and services using familiar names.

8. Network Security:

- Network security measures protect networks from unauthorized access, data breaches, and cyber-attacks. Common security mechanisms include firewalls, encryption, virtual private networks (VPNs), and authentication methods.

9. Network Types:

- Besides LAN and WAN, there are other specialized network types, such as Metropolitan Area Network (MAN), Campus Area Network (CAN), and Personal Area Network (PAN).

10. Network Services:

- Network services provide specific functionalities to network users. Examples include email, file sharing, printing, web hosting, and video conferencing.

11. Network Address Translation (NAT):

- NAT is a technique used to translate private IP addresses of devices within a LAN into a single public IP address when communicating with external networks (e.g., the internet).
- It allows multiple devices in the LAN to share a single public IP address, conserving the limited pool of public IP addresses.

12. Subnetting:

- Subnetting is the process of dividing a large IP network into smaller subnetworks or subnets. It helps manage IP address allocation and improves network efficiency and security.

13. Bandwidth and Throughput:

- Bandwidth refers to the maximum data transfer rate of a network connection, usually measured in bits per second (bps).
- Throughput is the actual data transfer rate experienced by users, which may be lower than the available bandwidth due to various factors like network congestion and protocol overhead.

14. Packet Switching:

- Packet switching is a method used to transmit data over a network in the form of discrete units called packets.
- Each packet contains a portion of the data, along with the destination address, allowing packets to take different routes to reach their destination.

15. Network Routing:

- Routing is the process of determining the best path for data packets to travel from the source to the destination across a network.
- Routers are devices responsible for making routing decisions based on the destination IP

address.

16. Network Addressing Modes:

- IP addresses can be assigned using different addressing modes, such as static IP addressing, dynamic IP addressing (DHCP), and automatic IP addressing (APIPA).

17. Network Congestion:

- Network congestion occurs when the volume of data traffic exceeds the network's capacity, leading to performance issues and delays.
- Congestion can be managed using techniques like traffic shaping and Quality of Service (QoS) to prioritize certain types of traffic.

18. Ethernet:

- Ethernet is a widely used technology for connecting devices in a LAN. It uses cables and switches to create a wired network infrastructure.

19. Wi-Fi (Wireless Fidelity):

- Wi-Fi enables wireless communication between devices using radio waves, allowing users to connect to a network without physical cables.

20. Network Troubleshooting:

- Network troubleshooting involves diagnosing and resolving issues related to network connectivity, performance, and security.
- Tools like ping, traceroute, and network analyzers are commonly used for troubleshooting.

21. Network Redundancy:

- Network redundancy involves creating backup or alternative paths in a network to ensure continuous connectivity in case of failure or disruptions.

22. Network Load Balancing:

- Load balancing distributes network traffic across multiple paths or devices to optimize resource utilization and prevent bottlenecks.

23. Virtual Local Area Network (VLAN):

- VLANs are logical subnetworks created within a physical LAN, allowing devices to communicate as if they were part of the same network, even if they are physically separate.

24. Point-to-Point Protocol (PPP):

- PPP is a data link layer protocol used to establish a direct connection between two devices, often used for dial-up internet connections and VPNs.

25. Network Monitoring and Management:

- Network administrators use monitoring and management tools to oversee network performance, security, and resource allocation.

Networking continues to advance with the growth of the internet, cloud computing, Internet of Things (IoT), and other emerging technologies. A strong understanding of networking concepts and protocols is essential for professionals in IT, telecommunications, and network administration to design, configure, and maintain robust and secure network infrastructures.

3.1 Network Devices and Technologies

In this section, we will explore various network devices and technologies commonly used in networking to facilitate communication, data transmission, and resource sharing.

1. **Network Router:**
   - A router is a networking device that connects different networks together, such as LANs and WANs, and forwards data packets between them.
   - Routers use IP addresses to make routing decisions and direct data packets to their destinations.

2. **Network Switch:**
   - A switch is a device that connects multiple devices within a LAN and forwards data packets only to the intended recipient.
   - Unlike hubs, switches create dedicated communication paths, improving network performance and reducing collisions.

3. **Network Hub:**
   - A hub is a basic networking device that connects multiple devices in a LAN, allowing them to communicate with each other.
   - Data received by a hub is broadcasted to all connected devices, which can cause collisions and reduce network efficiency.

4. **Network Access Point (NAP):**
   - A Network Access Point is a physical location where multiple ISPs (Internet Service Providers) connect their networks to exchange internet traffic.

5. **Modem:**
   - A modem (modulator-demodulator) is a device that converts digital data from a computer into analog signals for transmission over analog communication lines (e.g., telephone lines) and vice versa.
   - Modems are commonly used to provide internet access over DSL (Digital Subscriber Line) or

dial-up connections.

6. Network Firewall:

- A network firewall is a security device or software that monitors and controls incoming and outgoing network traffic, protecting the network from unauthorized access and cyber threats.

7. Network Access Controller (NAC):

- NAC is a technology that enforces security policies and authentication requirements for devices connecting to a network.

- It ensures that only authorized devices can access the network and may perform security checks before granting access.

8. Wireless Access Point (WAP):

- A wireless access point is a device that enables wireless devices (e.g., laptops, smartphones) to connect to a wired network using Wi-Fi technology.

9. Network Load Balancer:

- A network load balancer distributes network traffic across multiple servers or network paths to optimize resource utilization and ensure high availability.

10. Network Bridge:

- A network bridge connects two separate LANs to form a single logical network.

- It operates at the data link layer of the OSI model and forwards data packets based on MAC addresses.

11. Network Gateway:

- A network gateway is a device or software that serves as an entry and exit point between two different networks, translating data and protocols as needed.

12. Network Proxy Server:

- A proxy server acts as an intermediary between clients and servers, handling requests and responses on behalf of the clients.

- It can improve security, caching, and performance by reducing direct connections to external servers.

13. Virtual Private Network (VPN):

- A VPN is a secure, encrypted connection established over a public network (e.g., the internet) to allow remote users to access private networks as if they were connected locally.

14. Network Switch Stacking:

- Switch stacking involves connecting multiple switches together to form a single logical switch, allowing for easier management and increased capacity.

15. Quality of Service (QoS):

- QoS is a set of techniques used to prioritize certain types of network traffic over others to ensure better performance for critical applications (e.g., voice and video).

16. Network Proxy Server:

- A proxy server acts as an intermediary between clients and servers, handling requests and responses on behalf of the clients.
- It can improve security, caching, and performance by reducing direct connections to external servers.

17. Virtual Private Network (VPN):

- A VPN is a secure, encrypted connection established over a public network (e.g., the internet) to allow remote users to access private networks as if they were connected locally.

18. Network Switch Stacking:

- Switch stacking involves connecting multiple switches together to form a single logical switch, allowing for easier management and increased capacity.

19. Quality of Service (QoS):

- QoS is a set of techniques used to prioritize certain types of network traffic over others to ensure better performance for critical applications (e.g., voice and video).

20. Network Protocol Analyzer (Packet Sniffer):

- A network protocol analyzer, also known as a packet sniffer, captures and analyzes network traffic to troubleshoot network issues and monitor network performance.

21. Power over Ethernet (PoE):

- PoE technology allows network devices, such as IP cameras and wireless access points, to receive power and data over the same Ethernet cable, eliminating the need for separate power sources.

22. Network Virtualization:

- Network virtualization involves creating multiple virtual networks on a single physical network infrastructure, enabling better resource allocation and network management.

23. Software-Defined Networking (SDN):

- SDN is an approach to network management that separates the network's control plane from the data plane, allowing for centralized network control and dynamic configuration.

24. Network Attached Storage (NAS):

- NAS is a specialized storage device connected to a network that provides file-level data storage and sharing for multiple users and devices.

25. Voice over IP (VoIP):

- VoIP is a technology that allows voice communications over the internet, converting analog voice signals into digital data packets for transmission.

26. Cloud Computing:

- Cloud computing refers to the delivery of computing services, such as storage, processing power, and applications, over the internet (the cloud) rather than on local servers.

27. Software as a Service (SaaS):

- SaaS is a cloud computing model where software applications are provided over the internet, and users access them through a web browser without installing them locally.

28. Infrastructure as a Service (IaaS):

- IaaS is a cloud computing model that provides virtualized computing resources, such as virtual machines and storage, over the internet.

29. Platform as a Service (PaaS):

- PaaS is a cloud computing model that provides a platform and development environment for building, deploying, and managing applications over the internet.

30. Internet of Things (IoT):

- IoT refers to the network of interconnected devices, sensors, and objects that can collect and exchange data over the internet.
- IoT technology enables the integration of physical devices into digital systems to enable automation and data-driven decision-making.

31. Network Security Appliances:

- Network security appliances are specialized devices designed to provide advanced security functions, such as firewalling, intrusion detection/prevention, and content filtering.

32. Virtual LAN (VLAN):

- VLAN is a logical network created within a physical LAN to segregate devices into different broadcast domains.
- VLANs help improve security and network management by restricting communication between devices in different VLANs.

33. Voice VLAN:

- A voice VLAN is a specialized VLAN designed to carry voice traffic for VoIP systems separately from regular data traffic.

34. Software-Defined Wide Area Network (SD-WAN):

- SD-WAN is a software-defined approach to managing and optimizing wide area networks

(WANs) using centralized control and virtualization.

35. Remote Desktop Protocol (RDP):

- RDP is a protocol that allows users to connect to and control a remote computer or server over a network.
- It enables remote access and administration of computers.

36. Network Attached Storage (NAS):

- NAS is a specialized storage device connected to a network that provides file-level data storage and sharing for multiple users and devices.

37. Load Balancer:

- A load balancer distributes network traffic across multiple servers or resources to ensure optimal resource utilization and prevent overloading of individual components.

38. Network Time Protocol (NTP):

- NTP is a protocol used to synchronize the clocks of devices on a network to maintain accurate timekeeping and coordination.

39. Content Delivery Network (CDN):

- CDN is a network of distributed servers that cache and deliver web content, such as images, videos, and scripts, to users based on their geographic location.

40. Multiprotocol Label Switching (MPLS):

- MPLS is a protocol used to efficiently route data packets over a wide area network, providing high-performance and quality of service for data transmission.

41. Internet Service Provider (ISP):

- An ISP is a company that provides internet access to individuals and organizations, connecting them to the internet through various technologies.

42. Network Monitoring:

- Network monitoring involves observing network activities, performance, and status to detect and troubleshoot issues and optimize network resources.

43. Network Segmentation:

- Network segmentation is the practice of dividing a network into smaller, isolated segments to improve security and manage network traffic effectively.

44. Network Tunneling:

- Network tunneling is a technique that encapsulates data packets within another protocol to enable secure communication over an untrusted network, such as the internet.

45. Network Authentication:

- Network authentication verifies the identity of users and devices before allowing them access to the network, typically through username-password or certificate-based authentication.

46. Intranet and Extranet:

- An intranet is a private network within an organization that facilitates internal communication and collaboration among employees.

- An extranet is an extension of the intranet that allows authorized external parties, such as customers or partners, limited access to the organization's resources.

47. Network Address Translation (NAT):

- NAT is a technique that allows multiple devices on a private network to share a single public IP address for internet communication, providing an extra layer of security.

48. DHCP (Dynamic Host Configuration Protocol):

- DHCP is a network protocol used to automatically assign IP addresses and network configuration to devices joining a network.

49. Wireless Mesh Network:

- A wireless mesh network is a decentralized network where each device can relay data to other devices, creating a self-healing and robust network infrastructure.

50. 5G Network:

- 5G is the fifth generation of mobile network technology, offering higher data speeds, lower latency, and increased capacity compared to previous generations.

Networking devices and technologies play a pivotal role in building and managing modern networks, enabling seamless communication, data sharing, and resource utilization. As technology continues to evolve, networking remains at the forefront, supporting various industries and applications, including cloud computing, IoT, artificial intelligence, and smart cities. Understanding these devices and technologies is essential for IT professionals and network administrators to design, implement, and secure robust and efficient network infrastructures.

3.2 Cabling and Connectors

In networking, cabling and connectors are essential components that physically connect devices and facilitate data transmission between them. Different types of cables and connectors are used depending on the network topology, speed requirements, and distance between devices. Here are some common cabling types and connectors used in networking:

Cabling Types:

1. **Twisted Pair Cable:**
- Twisted pair cable consists of pairs of insulated copper wires twisted together to reduce electromagnetic interference and crosstalk.
- Two common categories of twisted pair cables are:
  - Unshielded Twisted Pair (UTP): Used in most Ethernet networks, including Cat5e, Cat6, and Cat6a cables.
  - Shielded Twisted Pair (STP): Offers additional protection against interference by adding a metal foil or braid shield around each pair.

2. **Coaxial Cable:**
- Coaxial cable features a central copper conductor surrounded by a dielectric insulator, a metal mesh or foil shield, and an outer jacket.
- It is commonly used for cable television (CATV) and some older Ethernet networks.

3. **Fiber Optic Cable:**
- Fiber optic cable uses thin strands of glass or plastic to transmit data as pulses of light, offering high-speed and long-distance data transmission.
- It is widely used in high-performance networks and long-distance connections.

Cabling Connectors:

1. **RJ-45 Connector:**
- The RJ-45 connector is commonly used with twisted pair Ethernet cables (e.g., Cat5e, Cat6) and is the standard connector for Ethernet networking.
- It has eight pins and is used for both data transmission and Power over Ethernet (PoE).

2. **BNC Connector:**
- The BNC (Bayonet Neill-Concelman) connector is used with coaxial cables, commonly found in older Ethernet networks and video applications.

3. **LC Connector:**
- The LC (Lucent Connector) connector is a small, push-and-latch type connector used with fiber optic cables.
- It is commonly used in high-speed fiber optic networks.

4. **SC Connector:**
- The SC (Subscriber Connector or Standard Connector) connector is another popular connector used with fiber optic cables.
- It features a push-pull mechanism for easy insertion and removal.

5. **ST Connector:**
- The ST (Straight Tip) connector is an older fiber optic connector that uses a bayonet-style twist-lock mechanism for secure connections.

6. **MT-RJ Connector:**
- The MT-RJ (Mechanical Transfer Registered Jack) connector is a duplex connector that combines both transmit and receive fibers in a single connector.

7. **USB Connector:**
- USB (Universal Serial Bus) connectors are used for various devices, including networking adapters, to connect to computers and other devices.

8. **HDMI Connector:**
- HDMI (High-Definition Multimedia Interface) connectors are used for audio and video connections in devices like TVs, monitors, and multimedia systems.

9. **VGA Connector:**
- The VGA (Video Graphics Array) connector is a standard analog video connector used for computer monitors and projectors.

10. **DisplayPort Connector:**
- The DisplayPort connector is used for high-definition video and audio connections between computers and monitors or display devices.

11. **MPO/MTP Connector:**
- The MPO (Multi-fiber Push-On) or MTP (Multi-fiber Termination Push-On) connector is used with high-density fiber optic cables that contain multiple fibers in a single connector.
- It is commonly used in data centers and high-speed fiber optic networks.

12. **SFP (Small Form-Factor Pluggable) Connector:**
- SFP connectors are used with SFP transceivers, which are hot-swappable modules used for various network connections, such as fiber optic or copper Ethernet connections.
- SFP connectors are commonly found in switches, routers, and network interface cards.

13. **RJ-11 Connector:**
- The RJ-11 connector is used with telephone cables and provides two to six pins, typically used for analog voice communication.

14. **RJ-12 Connector:**
- The RJ-12 connector is similar to the RJ-11 but has six pins, often used for digital phone systems and some networking applications.

15. **DB-9 and DB-25 Connectors:**

- DB-9 and DB-25 connectors are used with serial communication ports (RS-232) to connect devices like modems, printers, and legacy serial devices.

16. XLR Connector:

- XLR connectors are used primarily for professional audio applications, such as microphones and audio mixers.

17. Power Connectors (DC and AC):

- Power connectors are used to supply electrical power to various network devices, such as routers, switches, and access points.
- Common power connectors include barrel connectors, IEC connectors, and AC power cords.

18. F-Type Connector:

- The F-type connector is used with coaxial cables for television signals and cable modems.

19. QSFP (Quad Small Form-Factor Pluggable) Connector:

- The QSFP connector is used with high-speed data connections, typically in data center environments, and supports data rates of 40 Gbps or higher.

20. M12 Connector:

- M12 connectors are used in industrial networking applications and are known for their rugged design and resistance to environmental factors.

21. Power over Ethernet (PoE) Connector:

- PoE connectors allow both data and electrical power to be delivered over a single Ethernet cable to power devices like IP cameras and wireless access points.

22. Thunderbolt Connector:

- Thunderbolt connectors are used for high-speed data and video connections in devices like computers and external storage devices.

23. USB Type-C Connector:

- USB Type-C connectors are reversible, meaning they can be inserted in either orientation, and are used for various devices, including smartphones, laptops, and peripherals.

24. DIN Connector:

- DIN connectors are used in audio and video applications and are commonly found in professional audio equipment.

25. Euroblock Connector:

- Euroblock connectors are used for audio connections in commercial and industrial applications.

Proper cabling and connectors are crucial for ensuring reliable and efficient network communication. Different types of cables and connectors cater to specific networking needs, such as data transmission speed, distance, and environmental considerations. When designing or setting up a network, it is essential to choose the appropriate cabling and connectors based on the specific requirements of the network infrastructure and the devices involved. Additionally, following industry best practices for cable management, termination, and labeling can help maintain a neat and organized network setup and aid in future maintenance and troubleshooting.

3.3 Networking Protocols and Services

Networking protocols are sets of rules and conventions that govern how data is transmitted, received, and processed in a network. They ensure seamless communication and data exchange between devices and are essential for the functioning of networks. Additionally, networking services are software applications or functionalities that run on top of protocols to provide specific network-related features and capabilities. Here are some common networking protocols and services:

Networking Protocols:

1. **Transmission Control Protocol (TCP):**
   - TCP is a reliable, connection-oriented protocol used for data transmission over IP networks.
   - It ensures data integrity, error correction, and flow control by establishing a connection before data transfer and confirming receipt of packets.
2. **Internet Protocol (IP):**
   - IP is the fundamental network layer protocol used to route data packets between devices across the internet or a private network.
   - IPv4 (Internet Protocol version 4) and IPv6 (Internet Protocol version 6) are the most commonly used versions.
3. **User Datagram Protocol (UDP):**
   - UDP is a connectionless, unreliable protocol used for faster, lightweight data transmission without the overhead of TCP's reliability features.
   - It is commonly used for real-time applications like video streaming and online gaming.
4. **Internet Control Message Protocol (ICMP):**
   - ICMP is used to send error messages and operational information about the network, such as ping requests and responses.
5. **Hypertext Transfer Protocol (HTTP):**

- HTTP is the foundation of data communication for the World Wide Web, allowing clients (web browsers) to request web pages from servers.

6. **Simple Mail Transfer Protocol (SMTP):**

- SMTP is used to send outgoing email messages from the client to the mail server and to deliver messages between mail servers.

7. **File Transfer Protocol (FTP):**

- FTP is used for transferring files between a client and a server over a network, commonly used for website hosting and file sharing.

8. **Secure Shell (SSH):**

- SSH is a secure protocol used to provide secure remote access and control of devices over an insecure network.

9. **Domain Name System (DNS):**

- DNS translates human-readable domain names (e.g., www.example.com) into IP addresses to facilitate communication between devices.

10. **Dynamic Host Configuration Protocol (DHCP):**

- DHCP is used to automatically assign IP addresses and network configurations to devices on a network, simplifying network setup and management.

11. **Border Gateway Protocol (BGP):**

- BGP is an exterior gateway protocol used for routing data between autonomous systems on the internet.

12. **Simple Network Management Protocol (SNMP):**

- SNMP is used for managing and monitoring network devices and gathering data about their performance and status.

13. **Internet Group Management Protocol (IGMP):**

- IGMP is used by devices to join and leave multicast groups to receive multicast traffic.

14. **Extensible Messaging and Presence Protocol (XMPP):**

- XMPP is an open-source protocol used for instant messaging and presence information exchange.

15. **Secure Socket Layer (SSL) / Transport Layer Security (TLS):**

- SSL and TLS are cryptographic protocols that provide secure communication over a computer network, commonly used for secure web browsing (HTTPS) and email encryption.

16. **Internet Protocol Security (IPsec):**

- IPsec is a suite of protocols used to secure IP communication by encrypting and authenticating data at the IP layer, ensuring secure VPN connections and data transmission.

17. Point-to-Point Protocol (PPP):

- PPP is a data link layer protocol used for establishing direct connections between two devices, commonly used for dial-up internet connections and connecting to ISPs.

18. Internet Control Message Protocol version 6 (ICMPv6):

- ICMPv6 is an extension of ICMP used with IPv6 to provide network diagnostic and error reporting services.

19. Internet Group Management Protocol version 3 (IGMPv3):

- IGMPv3 is an enhanced version of IGMP used for managing multicast group membership in IPv4 and IPv6 networks.

20. Real-Time Transport Protocol (RTP):

- RTP is a protocol used for transmitting real-time audio and video data over IP networks, commonly used in Voice over IP (VoIP) and video conferencing applications.

21. Network Time Protocol version 6 (NTPv6):

- NTPv6 is an extension of NTP used with IPv6 to synchronize clocks and maintain accurate timekeeping in IPv6 networks.

Networking Services:

1. Domain Controller:

- A domain controller is a server that authenticates users and devices on a Windows Active Directory domain, managing user accounts, permissions, and policies.

2. Network File Sharing:

- Network file sharing services allow users to access shared files and folders stored on network-attached storage (NAS) devices or servers.

3. Virtual Private Network (VPN) Service:

- VPN services provide secure remote access to a private network over the internet, ensuring encrypted data transmission.

4. Network Time Protocol (NTP) Service:

- NTP services synchronize the clocks of devices on a network to maintain accurate timekeeping and coordination.

5. Network Print Server:

- A network print server manages and shares printers on a network, allowing multiple users to access and use shared printers.

6. Network Monitoring Service:

- Network monitoring services monitor network performance, detect issues, and provide alerts for quick troubleshooting and resolution.

7. Network Security Services:

- Network security services include firewalls, intrusion detection/prevention systems, and antivirus solutions to protect the network from unauthorized access and cyber threats.

8. Network Virtualization Service:

- Network virtualization services create virtual networks on a physical network infrastructure, providing better resource allocation and management.

9. Quality of Service (QoS) Service:

- QoS services prioritize network traffic to ensure the reliable transmission of critical applications and services.

10. Unified Communication (UC) Service:

- UC services integrate various communication channels (e.g., voice, video, messaging) into a single platform for efficient collaboration.

11. Network Backup and Recovery Service:

- Backup and recovery services automate the process of backing up data on the network to prevent data loss and facilitate recovery in case of hardware failures or disasters.

12. Network Authentication Service:

- Network authentication services manage user authentication and access control on the network, ensuring only authorized users can access resources.

13. Network Address Translation (NAT) Service:

- NAT services translate private IP addresses used within a local network to a single public IP address for internet communication, providing an additional layer of security.

14. Network Load Balancing Service:

- Load balancing services distribute network traffic across multiple servers or resources to ensure optimal resource utilization and prevent server overload.

15. Content Filtering Service:

- Content filtering services block or allow access to specific websites or content categories based on predefined policies, enhancing network security and compliance.

16. Network Intrusion Detection System (IDS) and Network Intrusion Prevention System (IPS):

- IDS and IPS services monitor network traffic for suspicious or malicious activities and can alert administrators or take preventive actions to protect the network.

17. Virtual Local Area Network (VLAN) Service:

- VLAN services create and manage virtual LANs, allowing network administrators to segment the network logically for better security and traffic management.

18. Network Acceleration and Optimization Service:

- These services use various techniques, such as caching and compression, to optimize network performance and reduce latency.

19. Software-Defined Networking (SDN) Service:

- SDN services leverage the SDN concept to enable centralized network management and dynamic configuration for efficient network operations.

20. Network Traffic Analysis Service:

- Traffic analysis services use advanced analytics to study network traffic patterns, detect anomalies, and identify potential security threats or performance issues.

21. Network Forensics Service:

- Network forensics services help investigate and analyze security incidents and network breaches to identify the root cause and prevent future occurrences.

22. Virtual Private LAN Service (VPLS):

- VPLS extends Ethernet LAN services across Wide Area Networks (WANs), allowing geographically dispersed sites to appear as a single LAN.

23. Software-Defined Wide Area Network (SD-WAN) Service:

- SD-WAN services use software-defined technology to manage and optimize wide area networks, providing flexibility and cost-efficiency.

24. Edge Computing Service:

- Edge computing services move data processing and storage closer to the edge of the network, reducing latency and enhancing performance for edge devices.

25. Mobile Device Management (MDM) Service:

- MDM services manage and secure mobile devices used in an organization, ensuring data protection and policy enforcement.

Networking protocols and services continue to evolve with technological advancements, shaping the way networks are designed, implemented, and managed. Each protocol and service serves a specific purpose and addresses different aspects of network communication, security, and performance. By leveraging the right protocols and services, network administrators can create efficient, secure, and reliable network infrastructures to support various applications and meet the needs of modern digital environments.

Quiz

1. What is the primary function of the CPU?

   a) Storage of data

   b) Execution of instructions

   c) Display of output

   d) Input of data

2. Which type of memory is non-volatile and retains data even when the power is turned off?

   a) RAM

   b) ROM

   c) Cache memory

   d) Virtual memory

3. What does BIOS stand for in a computer system?

   a) Basic Input Output System

   b) Basic Integrated Operating System

   c) Binary Input Output System

   d) Backup Input Output System

4. Which of the following is a secondary storage device?

   a) CPU

   b) RAM

   c) Hard Disk Drive

   d) Motherboard

5. What is the purpose of a network router?

   a) Connect devices within a LAN

   b) Connect devices to the internet

   c) Forward data packets between networks

   d) Store data in a network

6. Which network protocol is used for secure communication over the internet?

   a) HTTP

   b) FTP

   c) SSL/TLS

   d) SMTP

7. What is the function of a DNS server in a network?

   a) File sharing

b) Network monitoring

c) IP address assignment

d) Domain name to IP address resolution (Correct)

8. Which type of cable is commonly used for wired Ethernet networks?

   a) Twisted pair cable

   b) Fiber optic cable

   c) Coaxial cable

   d) USB cable

9. What does the acronym "LAN" stand for in networking?

   a) Local Access Network

   b) Long Area Network

   c) Local Area Network

   d) Logical Access Node

10. Which of the following is a wireless communication technology used for short-range data exchange?

    a) Wi-Fi

    b) Bluetooth

    c) Ethernet

    d) NFC

11. Which network protocol is used for sending email messages?

    a) HTTP

    b) SMTP

    c) FTP

    d) POP3

12. What is the maximum data transfer speed of a USB 3.0 port?

    a) 480 Mbps

    b) 1 Gbps

    c) 5 Gbps

    d) 10 Gbps

13. What is the default subnet mask for a Class C IP address?

    a) 255.0.0.0

    b) 255.255.0.0

    c) 255.255.255.0

d) 255.255.255.255

14. Which network topology connects all devices in a linear sequence?

    a) Bus

    b) Ring

    c) Star

    d) Linear (Correct)

15. What does the acronym "URL" stand for?

    a) Universal Resource Locator

    b) Universal Routing Label

    c) Uniform Routing Language

    d) Uniform Resource Language

16. Which protocol is used for transferring web pages from a web server to a web browser?

    a) FTP

    b) HTTP

    c) SMTP

    d) DNS

17. Which type of IP address is used for communication within a local network and not routable on the internet?

    a) Public IP address

    b) Dynamic IP address

    c) Private IP address

    d) Static IP address

18. What is the default port number for HTTP?

    a) 80

    b) 25

    c) 443

    d) 21

19. Which networking device forwards data packets between devices within a local network based on MAC addresses?

    a) Switch

    b) Router

    c) Hub

    d) Modem

20. Which wireless encryption protocol provides the highest level of security?

    a) WEP

    b) WPA

    c) WPA2

    d) WPS

21. What is the purpose of a firewall in a network?

    a) Speed up data transmission

    b) Prevent unauthorized access and protect against cyber threats

    c) Increase network storage capacity

    d) Monitor network traffic

22. Which of the following is a multicast routing protocol?

    a) BGP

    b) OSPF

    c) IGMP

    d) RIP

23. What does the acronym "VoIP" stand for in networking?

    a) Voice over Internet Protocol

    b) Video over IP

    c) Virtual Office Internet Phone

    d) Voice of IP

24. Which network service is responsible for translating domain names into IP addresses?

    a) DHCP

    b) NTP

    c) DNS

    d) FTP

25. What is the maximum data transfer rate of a Gigabit Ethernet connection?

    a) 10 Mbps

    b) 100 Mbps

    c) 1 Gbps

    d) 10 Gbps

26. What is the purpose of an Access Point (AP) in a wireless network?

    a) Forward data packets between different networks

    b) Assign IP addresses to devices on the network

c) Provide wireless connectivity and act as a central hub for wireless devices

d) Establish secure VPN connections

27. Which of the following is a protocol used for secure remote access to a network?

    a) HTTP

    b) SSH

    c) SMTP

    d) FTP

28. What is the purpose of the "ping" command in networking?

    a) Test the speed of the internet connection

    b) Transfer files between computers

    c) Check the connectivity to a remote host

    d) Monitor network traffic

29. Which network service automatically assigns IP addresses to devices when they connect to a network?

    a) DHCP

    b) DNS

    c) FTP

    d) HTTP

30. Which protocol is responsible for sending email messages from a mail client to a mail server?

    a) POP3

    b) SMTP

    c) IMAP

    d) HTTP

Mobile Devices

Mobile devices are portable electronic gadgets designed for communication, information retrieval, and various other tasks on the go. These devices have become an integral part of modern life, enabling users to stay connected, work, and entertain themselves wherever they are. Mobile devices come in various forms, including smartphones, tablets, and wearable devices. Here are some key aspects of mobile devices:

1. **Smartphones:**

Smartphones are advanced mobile phones that offer features beyond voice calling and text messaging.

They typically have touchscreens, internet connectivity, and access to mobile applications (apps).

Smartphones run on operating systems such as Android, iOS, and Windows.

2. **Tablets:**

Tablets are portable computing devices with larger screens than smartphones but more compact than laptops.

They are primarily used for web browsing, media consumption, and productivity tasks.

Tablets can run on the same operating systems as smartphones.

3. **Wearable Devices:**

Wearable devices are gadgets worn on the body, often in the form of smartwatches, fitness trackers, and augmented reality glasses.

They offer features like health tracking, notifications, and hands-free access to information.

4. **Mobile Apps:**

Mobile devices rely on applications or apps to provide various functionalities and services.

App stores offer a wide range of apps, including social media, productivity tools, games, and more.

5. **Internet Connectivity:**

Mobile devices connect to the internet using cellular data (3G, 4G, 5G) or Wi-Fi networks.

Internet access allows users to browse the web, use cloud-based services, and access online content.

6. **Location Services:**

Mobile devices often have GPS capabilities, enabling location-based services like maps, navigation, and location-aware apps.

7. Mobile Payment:

Many mobile devices support mobile payment services, allowing users to make purchases using their smartphones or wearables.

8. Biometric Security:

Mobile devices may incorporate biometric authentication, such as fingerprint sensors or facial recognition, for enhanced security.

9. Battery Life:

Battery life is crucial for mobile devices to ensure they can be used throughout the day without frequent charging.

10. Mobile Operating Systems:

Different mobile devices run on various operating systems, with Android and iOS being the most popular.

11. Cloud Integration:

Mobile devices often integrate with cloud services, allowing seamless access to files and data across devices.

12. Mobile Gaming:

Mobile devices offer a vast array of gaming options, from casual games to high-quality, immersive experiences.

13. Mobile Photography:

Mobile devices, especially smartphones, have become popular tools for photography.

Built-in cameras with high resolution and advanced features allow users to capture high-quality photos and videos.

14. Mobile Communication Apps:

Mobile devices offer a wide range of communication apps, such as messaging apps, video conferencing apps, and social media platforms.

These apps enable real-time communication with friends, family, and colleagues.

15. Mobile Health and Fitness Apps:

Many mobile devices come with health and fitness tracking capabilities and support various health and fitness apps.

These apps can monitor physical activity, heart rate, sleep patterns, and provide personalized fitness plans.

16. Mobile Entertainment:

Mobile devices serve as portable entertainment centers, offering access to streaming services, music, movies, and games.

17. Mobile Productivity Apps:

Mobile devices support productivity apps, including word processors, spreadsheets, note-taking apps, and cloud-based collaboration tools.

These apps enable users to work on documents and projects while on the move.

18. Mobile E-commerce:

Mobile devices have revolutionized e-commerce, allowing users to shop online, make payments, and track orders from their smartphones or tablets.

19. Mobile Virtual Assistants:

Virtual assistants like Siri (iOS) and Google Assistant (Android) are integrated into many mobile devices.

They provide voice-based assistance and perform tasks based on user commands.

20. Mobile Gaming Accessories:

Mobile gaming has led to the development of various gaming accessories, such as controllers and external cooling fans, to enhance the gaming experience.

21. Mobile Device Management (MDM):

Mobile Device Management solutions are used by businesses to manage and secure company-owned mobile devices.

MDM helps enforce security policies, configure devices, and remotely manage apps and data.

22. Mobile Hotspot:

Many smartphones and tablets can act as mobile hotspots, providing internet connectivity to other devices through Wi-Fi.

23. Mobile Wallets:

Mobile wallets store payment card information securely on mobile devices, allowing users to make contactless payments at supported merchants.

24. Mobile Augmented Reality (AR) and Virtual Reality (VR):

Mobile devices support AR and VR experiences through dedicated apps and accessories, providing immersive and interactive content.

25. Mobile Accessibility Features:

Mobile devices offer accessibility features for users with disabilities, such as screen readers, magnification, and voice control.

26. Mobile Security:

Mobile security is essential to protect against data breaches, malware, and unauthorized access.

Users are encouraged to use strong passwords, enable biometric authentication, and keep their devices and apps up to date.

27. Mobile Device Recycling and Sustainability:

As mobile devices are constantly upgraded, recycling programs and sustainability initiatives are becoming more important to reduce electronic waste.

28. Mobile Satellite Communication:

Some specialized mobile devices support satellite communication, providing connectivity in remote and isolated areas.

29. Mobile Multitasking:

Mobile devices offer multitasking capabilities, allowing users to switch between apps and perform multiple tasks simultaneously.

30. Mobile Banking and Finance:

Mobile banking apps enable users to manage their finances, check account balances, transfer funds, and pay bills conveniently.

4.1 Laptops and Mobile Devices

Laptops and mobile devices are portable computing devices that have revolutionized the way people work, communicate, and access information. While laptops are more traditional portable computers, mobile devices encompass a broader category, including smartphones, tablets, and wearable gadgets. Let's delve into the features and characteristics of laptops and mobile devices:

Laptops:

1. **Portability:** Laptops are designed to be portable and lightweight, allowing users to carry them around easily.
2. **Form Factor:** Laptops consist of a keyboard, touchpad or trackpad, and a built-in display, all integrated into a single unit.
3. **Performance:** Laptops are equipped with processors, RAM, and storage similar to desktop computers, providing decent computing power for a wide range of tasks.
4. **Operating Systems:** Laptops run operating systems like Windows, macOS, or Linux, offering a full-fledged computing experience with a wide variety of software applications.
5. **Battery Life:** While battery life can vary, modern laptops offer several hours of usage without requiring constant charging.
6. **Connectivity:** Laptops typically have multiple ports, including USB, HDMI, audio jacks, and sometimes Ethernet, allowing users to connect various peripherals.
7. **Multitasking:** Laptops support multitasking, enabling users to run multiple applications simultaneously.
8. **Productivity:** Laptops are commonly used for work-related tasks, content creation, and professional use.
9. **Gaming:** High-performance laptops with dedicated graphics cards can handle gaming and multimedia tasks.
10. **Form Factors:** Laptops come in various form factors, including traditional clamshell designs and 2-in-1 convertible laptops that can be used as both a laptop and a tablet.
11. **Screen Size:** Laptops typically have larger screens than mobile devices, ranging from around 11 to 17 inches, providing a more immersive viewing experience.
12. **Storage:** Laptops offer larger storage capacities than most mobile devices, with options for traditional hard disk drives (HDDs) or faster solid-state drives (SSDs).
13. **Input Methods:** Laptops have physical keyboards, which are beneficial for tasks involving

extensive typing and data entry.

14. **Productivity Software:** Laptops are favored for professional use due to their compatibility with full-fledged productivity software such as Microsoft Office and Adobe Creative Suite.

Mobile Devices:

1. **Variety:** Mobile devices include a range of portable gadgets, such as smartphones, tablets, smartwatches, and fitness trackers.
2. **Touchscreen Interface:** Most mobile devices feature touchscreens, allowing users to interact directly with the display.
3. **Operating Systems:** Mobile devices use specific mobile operating systems, such as Android and iOS, tailored for touch-based interactions and app ecosystems.
4. **Apps and Ecosystems:** Mobile devices heavily rely on mobile applications (apps) for various tasks and entertainment. App stores offer a vast selection of apps for download.
5. **Connectivity:** Mobile devices connect to the internet using cellular data (3G, 4G, 5G) or Wi-Fi networks.
6. **Portability:** Mobile devices are designed for ultimate portability, fitting easily in pockets or bags.
7. **Battery Life:** Battery life can vary based on usage, but most mobile devices require frequent charging due to their compact size.
8. **Communication:** Mobile devices excel in communication, providing voice calls, messaging, and social media access.
9. **Location Services:** Built-in GPS allows mobile devices to provide location-based services like maps and navigation.
10. **Wearable Devices:** Some mobile devices, like smartwatches and fitness trackers, are worn on the body and offer specialized functions like health tracking and notifications.
11. **Mobile Payments:** Mobile devices support mobile payment services, enabling contactless transactions via digital wallets.
12. **Photography:** Smartphones, in particular, are renowned for their high-quality built-in cameras, making mobile devices popular for photography and video recording.
13. **Always-On Connectivity:** Mobile devices are always connected to the internet, enabling real-time access to information, notifications, and social media.
14. **App Ecosystem:** Mobile devices rely heavily on apps to provide a wide range of functionalities, from productivity tools to entertainment and games.

15. **Customization:** Users can personalize their mobile devices with different themes, wallpapers, and app layouts to suit their preferences.

16. **Social Connectivity:** Mobile devices are essential for social networking, allowing users to stay connected with friends, family, and colleagues through messaging and social media apps.

17. **Instant Communication:** Mobile devices enable instant communication through voice calls, video calls, and messaging, enhancing real-time collaboration and communication.

18. **Mobile Payment Services:** Mobile devices facilitate contactless payments using services like Apple Pay, Google Pay, Samsung Pay, and others.

19. **Mobile Gaming:** Mobile devices are a popular platform for casual gaming, with a vast selection of games available on app stores.

20. **Digital Wallets:** Mobile devices store digital versions of credit cards, loyalty cards, boarding passes, and tickets, reducing the need for physical cards and paper documents.

21. **Fitness and Health Tracking:** Many mobile devices feature built-in health and fitness tracking capabilities, helping users monitor their physical activity and overall well-being.

22. **Augmented Reality (AR) and Virtual Reality (VR):** Mobile devices support AR and VR experiences through dedicated apps and accessories, opening up new possibilities for interactive content.

23. **Mobile Accessories:** Various accessories are available for mobile devices, including cases, portable chargers, Bluetooth earbuds, and camera lenses.

24. **Cloud Integration:** Mobile devices often integrate with cloud services, allowing seamless access to files and data across multiple devices.

25. **Multimedia Consumption:** Mobile devices are popular for multimedia consumption, including streaming videos, listening to music, and reading e-books.

The combination of laptops and mobile devices has transformed the way people work, communicate, and entertain themselves. Users can seamlessly transition from desktop computing on laptops to on-the-go mobility and communication with mobile devices. The versatility and integration of laptops and mobile devices have shaped a modern digital lifestyle, where individuals can stay connected and productive from virtually anywhere. As technology continues to advance, these devices are expected to become even more powerful, feature-rich, and interconnected, further enhancing the overall user experience.

4.2 Mobile OS and Applications

Mobile operating systems (OS) and applications are fundamental components that drive the functionaliy and user experience of mobile devices. Let's explore mobile OS and applicantions in more detail:

Mobile Operating Systems:

1. **Android:**
   - Developed by Google, Android is the most widely used mobile operating system globally.
   - It is an open-source OS, allowing device manufacturers to customize and adapt it for their hardware.
   - Android supports a vast ecosystem of apps available through the Google Play Store.
   - Key features include customizable home screens, notification center, and integration with Google services.

2. **iOS:**
   - Developed by Apple, iOS is exclusive to Apple's devices, including iPhones and iPads.
   - iOS offers a seamless integration with Apple's hardware and software ecosystem.
   - It provides a controlled and curated app environment through the Apple App Store.
   - Key features include an intuitive user interface, regular updates, and strong security measures.

3. **Windows Mobile (Discontinued):**
   - Windows Mobile was developed by Microsoft for smartphones and Pocket PCs.
   - However, Windows Mobile has been largely replaced by Windows Phone and later evolved into Windows 10 Mobile.
   - As of my last knowledge update in September 2021, Windows Mobile had been discontinued, and Microsoft shifted its focus to other areas.

4. **BlackBerry OS (Discontinued):**
   - Developed by BlackBerry Limited (formerly Research In Motion), BlackBerry OS was once prevalent in BlackBerry devices.
   - However, BlackBerry OS has been largely replaced by BlackBerry 10 and other platforms.
   - As of my last knowledge update in September 2021, BlackBerry OS was largely discontinued and no longer actively developed.

5. **Other Mobile OS:**
   - There are other mobile operating systems like KaiOS (for feature phones), Tizen (developed by Samsung), and HarmonyOS (developed by Huawei), catering to specific device categories or markets.

6. **KaiOS:**

- KaiOS is a lightweight mobile operating system designed primarily for feature phones and low-end smartphones.
- It focuses on providing essential smartphone features and internet connectivity to devices with limited hardware resources.
- KaiOS supports apps from the KaiStore, offering a range of popular apps and services to users of affordable devices.

7. **Tizen:**
- Tizen is an open-source operating system developed by the Linux Foundation and backed by Samsung and other partners.
- It is used in a variety of devices, including smartphones, smart TVs, smartwatches, and smart home appliances.
- Tizen offers a customizable user interface and supports both native and web apps.

8. **HarmonyOS (Hongmeng OS):**
- HarmonyOS, developed by Huawei, is a cross-device operating system designed to work across smartphones, tablets, smart TVs, wearables, and IoT devices.
- It focuses on a seamless and consistent user experience across different devices, enabling smooth device interactions and collaboration.

Mobile Applications:

1. **App Stores:** Mobile applications, commonly known as apps, are software programs designed specifically for mobile devices.
- Apps can be downloaded from official app stores like Google Play Store (for Android) and Apple App Store (for iOS).
- App stores offer various categories of apps, including games, productivity tools, social networking, health, and entertainment apps.

2. **Native Apps:**
- Native apps are developed for a specific mobile platform (e.g., Android or iOS) using platform-specific programming languages (Java/Kotlin for Android, Swift/Objective-C for iOS).
- Native apps have direct access to device features and provide a rich and optimized user experience.

3. **Web Apps:**
- Web apps are accessed through a web browser on the mobile device.
- They are platform-independent and do not require installation from an app store.

- Web apps often utilize responsive design to adapt to different screen sizes.

4. **Hybrid Apps:**
- Hybrid apps combine elements of both native and web apps.
- They are developed using web technologies (HTML, CSS, JavaScript) but run within a native container.
- Hybrid apps can access certain device features, and their development process is often more cost-effective.

5. **App Permissions:**
- Mobile apps require user permission to access certain device features, such as camera, location, contacts, and notifications.
- Users have the option to grant or deny these permissions during app installation or use.

6. **App Updates:**
- App developers release updates to add new features, improve performance, and fix bugs.
- App updates are available through the respective app stores.

7. **In-App Purchases and Monetization:**
- Many apps offer in-app purchases for additional features or content.
- App developers may monetize their apps through advertising, subscription models, or one-time purchases.

8. **Social Networking Apps:**
- Social networking apps like Facebook, Instagram, Twitter, LinkedIn, and Snapchat connect users with friends, family, and the broader online community.
- These apps offer various features, including sharing posts, photos, videos, and real-time messaging.

9. **Health and Fitness Apps:**
- Health and fitness apps track users' physical activity, exercise routines, sleep patterns, and nutritional intake.
- They help users set fitness goals, monitor progress, and maintain a healthy lifestyle.

10. **Entertainment Apps:**
- Entertainment apps include streaming services like Netflix, YouTube, Spotify, and Apple Music, providing users with access to a vast library of movies, TV shows, music, and podcasts.

11. **Gaming Apps:**
- Mobile gaming apps cover a wide range of genres, from casual games like puzzles and arcade

games to more complex and immersive games with console-like experiences.

- In-app purchases and ads are common revenue streams for mobile game developers.

12. **Productivity and Office Apps:**

- Productivity apps such as Microsoft Office Suite (Word, Excel, PowerPoint), Google Workspace, and note-taking apps enhance users' ability to work on documents, spreadsheets, and presentations on the go.

13. **Messaging Apps:**

- Messaging apps like WhatsApp, Facebook Messenger, and Telegram enable real-time text messaging, voice calls, and video calls, fostering seamless communication across distances.

14. **Navigation and Mapping Apps:**

- Navigation apps like Google Maps and Apple Maps offer turn-by-turn directions, traffic information, and location-based services to help users navigate and discover places.

15. **Camera and Photo Editing Apps:**

- Camera apps offer a range of features, filters, and effects to enhance mobile photography.
- Photo editing apps allow users to edit and retouch images directly on their devices.

16. **E-commerce Apps:**

1. E-commerce apps like Amazon, eBay, and Alibaba provide users with a convenient platform to shop for products and services online.

17. **Banking and Finance Apps:**

2. Banking apps enable users to manage their accounts, transfer funds, pay bills, and access financial services securely from their mobile devices.

18. **Ride-Sharing and Food Delivery Apps:**

3. Ride-sharing apps like Uber and Lyft and food delivery apps like Uber Eats and DoorDash have revolutionized transportation and food services, providing convenient on-demand services to users.

Mobile operating systems and applications continue to evolve rapidly, driven by technological advancements and user demands. The diversity of mobile apps caters to users' diverse needs and preferences, making mobile devices indispensable tools for various aspects of daily life. As mobile technology progresses, we can expect even more innovation in mobile OS, applications, and the overall mobile ecosystem.

4.3 Network Connectivity and Email

Network Connectivity:

Network connectivity is crucial for mobile devices to access the internet, communicate with other devices, and use various online services. Mobile devices utilize different network technologies to establish connections:

1. **Cellular Networks:**
- Mobile devices connect to cellular networks (3G, 4G, 5G) provided by mobile carriers.
- Cellular networks offer wide-area coverage and high-speed data access, enabling internet browsing, social media, video streaming, and more.
- The network technology (e.g., LTE, 5G) determines the speed and capabilities of the mobile data connection.

2. **Wi-Fi Networks:**
- Mobile devices can connect to Wi-Fi networks provided by routers or access points.
- Wi-Fi networks offer faster data transfer speeds and are commonly used in homes, offices, public places, and Wi-Fi hotspots.
- When connected to Wi-Fi, mobile devices can access the internet and local network resources.

3. **Bluetooth:**
- Bluetooth is used for short-range wireless communication between devices.
- Mobile devices use Bluetooth to connect to peripherals like wireless headphones, speakers, keyboards, and fitness trackers.

4. **NFC (Near Field Communication):**
- NFC enables contactless communication between devices when they are brought close together.
- It is used for quick data exchange, mobile payments, and pairing devices.

5. **Mobile Hotspot:**
- Mobile devices with cellular data can act as mobile hotspots, providing internet connectivity to other devices via Wi-Fi.

6. **VPN (Virtual Private Network):**
- Mobile devices can use VPNs to establish secure connections to remote networks, ensuring data privacy and security.

Email:

Email remains a fundamental means of communication, both in personal and professional contexts. Mobile devices support email access through dedicated email apps or web-based interfaces:

1. **Email Apps:**
- Mobile devices come with pre-installed email apps, such as Gmail (for Android) and Mail (for iOS).
- These apps allow users to configure multiple email accounts and access emails directly on the device.

2. **Web-based Email:**
- Users can also access email accounts through web browsers on their mobile devices.
- Web-based email services like Gmail, Outlook, and Yahoo Mail offer full access to email features and settings.

3. **Push Email:**
- Mobile devices support push email, where new messages are delivered instantly to the device as they arrive on the email server.
- This ensures real-time email synchronization without the need for manual refreshing.

4. **Email Synchronization:**
- Mobile devices sync emails across devices, ensuring that read, sent, and deleted messages are consistent on all devices.

5. **Attachments and File Sharing:**
- Email apps support attachments, allowing users to send and receive files, images, and documents with their emails.

6. **Email Security:**
- Mobile email apps use encryption and authentication to ensure secure communication between the device and the email server.
- Users are encouraged to set up device passcodes or biometric authentication to protect email access.

Mobile devices have made email communication more accessible and convenient, enabling users to stay connected and respond to messages even while on the move. The combination of network connectivity and email services has transformed mobile devices into powerful communication tools, allowing users to maintain productivity and responsiveness no matter where they are. As mobile networks continue to advance, email services will continue to play a significant role in mobile communications and remote collaboration.

Email Protocols:

Behind the scenes, email communication relies on various protocols to facilitate the exchange of messages between email clients and email servers:

1. **SMTP (Simple Mail Transfer Protocol):**
*   SMTP is the protocol used to send outgoing emails from an email client to the email server for delivery to the recipients' mail servers.
*   It defines the rules for message transmission and delivery.

2. **POP3 (Post Office Protocol version 3):**
*   POP3 is an email retrieval protocol that allows email clients to download emails from the server to the device.
*   Once downloaded, emails are typically removed from the server.

3. **IMAP (Internet Message Access Protocol):**
*   IMAP is another email retrieval protocol that enables email clients to synchronize emails with the server without downloading them.
*   It allows users to access their emails from multiple devices while keeping them stored on the server.

Email Security:

Email security is of paramount importance to protect sensitive information and prevent unauthorized access to email accounts:

1. **Secure Socket Layer (SSL) / Transport Layer Security (TLS):**
*   SSL/TLS encryption ensures secure communication between the email client and the email server, preventing interception of emails during transmission.

2. **Email Encryption:**
*   Users can use end-to-end email encryption to protect the content of their emails from unauthorized access.
*   Various encryption methods, such as PGP (Pretty Good Privacy) or S/MIME (Secure/Multipurpose Internet Mail Extensions), are available for enhanced email security.

3. **Two-Factor Authentication (2FA):**
*   Enabling 2FA adds an extra layer of security to email accounts by requiring a second form of verification (e.g., a unique code sent to the user's mobile device) during login.

4. **Spam and Phishing Protection:**

- Email providers implement spam filters and phishing protection to prevent unwanted and potentially harmful emails from reaching users' inboxes.

Mobile Email Best Practices:

To ensure a safe and efficient email experience on mobile devices, consider these best practices:

- **Use Strong Passwords:** Set strong, unique passwords for email accounts to prevent unauthorized access.
- **Update Device and Apps:** Keep your mobile device's operating system and email apps up-to-date to ensure you have the latest security patches.
- **Avoid Public Wi-Fi for Sensitive Emails:** Avoid accessing sensitive emails on public Wi-Fi networks to protect against potential security risks.
- **Backup Important Emails:** Regularly backup important emails to avoid data loss in case of device issues or accidental deletion.
- **Avoid Clicking Suspicious Links:** Be cautious of clicking links in emails from unknown or untrusted sources to avoid falling victim to phishing attacks.
- **Use Secure Email Apps:** Use official email apps or trusted third-party apps that support encryption and security features.
- **Log Out of Email Accounts:** Log out of email accounts when not in use to prevent unauthorized access, especially on shared devices.

Mobile devices have become indispensable tools for email communication, enabling users to stay connected to their personal and professional networks from virtually anywhere. By understanding and implementing email security measures and best practices, users can ensure a secure and seamless email experience on their mobile devices.

Quiz

1. **Question: What is the primary function of the CPU in a computer system?**

   A. Display graphics on the monitor

   B. Store data and files

   C. Execute instructions and perform calculations

   D. Provide internet connectivity

2. **Question: Which of the following is a volatile memory used for temporary data storage in a computer?**

   A. ROM (Read-Only Memory)

   B. HDD (Hard Disk Drive)

   C. RAM (Random Access Memory)

   D. SSD (Solid State Drive)

3. **Question: The motherboard is the main circuit board of a computer, and it connects various components. Which component is NOT typically directly connected to the motherboard?**

   A. CPU (Central Processing Unit)

   B. GPU (Graphics Processing Unit)

   C. RAM (Random Access Memory)

   D. HDD (Hard Disk Drive)

4. **Question: What is the purpose of the BIOS in a computer system?**

   A. Execute software applications

   B. Manage power supply to the components

   C. Provide a user interface for the operating system

   D. Initialize hardware and boot the operating system

5. **Question: Which of the following is a solid-state storage device used to store data even when the power is turned off?**

   A. RAM (Random Access Memory)

   B. HDD (Hard Disk Drive)

   C. SSD (Solid State Drive)

   D. ROM (Read-Only Memory)

6. **Question: Which type of peripheral is used to input text, numbers, and commands into a computer?**

   A. Monitor

B. Keyboard

C. Printer

D. Headphones

7. **Question: Which type of peripheral is used to produce hard copies of documents and images from a computer?**

A. Monitor

B. Keyboard

C. Printer

D. Headphones

8. **Question: What is the function of a router in a network?**

A. Connect devices within the same local area network (LAN)

B. Provide internet access to multiple devices in a LAN

C. Amplify the strength of Wi-Fi signals

D. Connect devices to the internet through a cellular network

9. **Question: What type of cable is commonly used to connect a computer to a wired Ethernet network?**

A. HDMI

B. USB

C. VGA

D. Ethernet

10. **Question: Which networking protocol is used to retrieve emails from a mail server to a client device?**

A. SMTP

B. POP3

C. IMAP

D. FTP

11. **Question: What does the acronym "WLAN" stand for?**

A. Wireless Local Area Network

B. Wide Area Local Network

C. Wired Local Access Network

D. Wireless Wide Area Local Network

12. **Question: Which wireless technology is used for short-range communication between devices, such as transferring files or making mobile payments?**

A. Bluetooth

B. Wi-Fi

C. NFC (Near Field Communication)

D. GPS (Global Positioning System)

13. **Question: Which mobile operating system is developed by Google and is commonly used in smartphones and tablets?**

A. Android

B. iOS

C. Windows Mobile

D. BlackBerry OS

14. **Question: Which mobile operating system is exclusive to Apple's iPhones and iPads?**

A. Android

B. iOS

C. Windows Mobile

D. BlackBerry OS

15. **Question: What is the purpose of an email protocol like SMTP?**

A. Access email from the server to the client

B. Send outgoing emails from the client to the server

C. Synchronize emails across multiple devices

D. Encrypt email messages for security

16. **Question: Which of the following is NOT a type of email protocol?**

A. SMTP

B. POP3

C. IMAP

D. HTTP

17. **Question: What is the purpose of SSL/TLS encryption in email communication?**

A. Securely access email from multiple devices

B. Protect email attachments from viruses

C. Prevent unauthorized access to the email server

D. Ensure secure communication between email client and server

18. **Question: Which type of email attachment allows users to encrypt the content of their emails for added security?**

A. ZIP files

B. Image files (JPEG, PNG)

C. PDF files

D. Encrypted files (PGP, S/MIME)

19. **Question: Which network technology provides the fastest mobile data transfer speeds?**

    A. 3G

    B. 4G

    C. 5G

    D. Wi-Fi

20. **Question: Which of the following is used for short-range wireless communication between devices like wireless headphones and keyboards?**

    A. Bluetooth

    B. NFC

    C. Wi-Fi

    D. Ethernet

21. **Question: Which component of a computer is responsible for displaying graphics on the monitor?**

    A. CPU

    B. GPU

    C. RAM

    D. Motherboard

22. **Question: What is the purpose of the BIOS in a computer system?**

    A. Control the flow of electricity to the components

    B. Execute software applications and games

    C. Initialize hardware and boot the operating system

    D. Connect peripherals to the computer

23. **Question: Which type of storage device is non-volatile and retains data even when the power is turned off?**

    A. RAM

    B. SSD

    C. HDD

    D. ROM

24. **Question: Which type of network allows computers and devices to communicate within a limited geographical area, like a home or office?**

A. LAN (Local Area Network)

B. WAN (Wide Area Network)

C. MAN (Metropolitan Area Network)

D. PAN (Personal Area Network)

25. **Question: What type of cable is commonly used to connect peripherals like printers and scanners to a computer?**

    A. HDMI

    B. USB

    C. Ethernet

    D. VGA

26. **Question: Which of the following is a common network topology where each device is connected to a central node?**

    A. Bus

    B. Star

    C. Ring

    D. Mesh

27. **Question: Which network device is used to forward data between different networks in an IP-based network?**

    A. Switch

    B. Router

    C. Hub

    D. Modem

28. **Question: Which networking protocol is commonly used for retrieving web pages and resources from the internet?**

    A. FTP (File Transfer Protocol)

    B. HTTP (Hypertext Transfer Protocol)

    C. DNS (Domain Name System)

    D. DHCP (Dynamic Host Configuration Protocol)

29. **Question: Which wireless technology is used for connecting devices to the internet within a limited area, such as a home or office?**

    A. Bluetooth

    B. NFC

    C. Wi-Fi

D. LTE

30. **Question: Which of the following is a portable computing device with a touchscreen interface, designed for media consumption and communication?**

A. Laptop

B. Smartphone

C. Desktop PC

D. Gaming Console

Hardware and Network Troubleshooting

Hardware and network troubleshooting are essential skills for identifying and resolving issues related to computer hardware components and network connectivity. Here are some common troubleshooting steps for hardware and network-related problems:

Hardware Troubleshooting:

1. **Check Power and Connections:**

Ensure that all devices are properly connected to power sources and turned on.

Check cables and connections for any damage or loose connections.

2. **Check Indicator Lights:**

Many devices have indicator lights that provide valuable information about their status.

Check for any error codes or warning lights on devices like routers, printers, or storage devices.

3. **Run Built-in Diagnostics:**

Some hardware components, like hard drives and memory, have built-in diagnostic tools.

Run hardware diagnostics to identify potential issues.

4. **Test Hardware in Another System:**

If possible, test the malfunctioning hardware (e.g., RAM, hard drive) in another compatible system to see if the issue persists.

5. **Update Drivers and Firmware:**

Ensure that all hardware drivers and firmware are up to date to avoid compatibility issues.

6. **Check for Overheating:**

Overheating can cause hardware failures. Monitor the system's temperature and clean dust from fans and vents.

7. **Check Device Manager (Windows) or System Information (Mac):**

Use these tools to identify any hardware devices with issues and update drivers if necessary.

8. **Run Memory and Disk Checks:**

Use tools like Windows Memory Diagnostic or macOS Disk Utility to check for memory and disk errors.

9. **Remove Recently Installed Hardware/Software:**

If the issue started after installing new hardware or software, consider removing it to see if the problem resolves.

10. **Check for Physical Damage:**

Inspect hardware components, such as cables, connectors, and ports, for physical damage or signs of wear.

11. **Check Power Supply:**

If a device is not powering on, check the power supply, power cable, and power outlet.

12. **Check External Devices:**

Disconnect external devices one by one (e.g., printers, external hard drives) to check if any of them are causing conflicts or issues.

13. **Boot into Safe Mode:**

Boot the computer into Safe Mode (Windows) or Safe Boot (Mac) to check if the problem persists in a minimal system configuration.

14. **Run Hardware Diagnostics Tools:**

Many computer manufacturers provide diagnostic tools that can help identify hardware problems, such as Dell Diagnostics, HP PC Hardware Diagnostics, or Apple Diagnostics.

15. **Reseat Hardware Components:**

Reseat components like RAM modules, expansion cards, and data cables to ensure they are properly connected.

Network Troubleshooting:

1. **Restart Devices:**

Power cycle the router, modem, and connected devices to resolve temporary network issues.

2. **Check Network Connections:**

Verify that all network cables are securely connected to devices and the network infrastructure.

3. **Ping Test:**

Use the ping command to check the connectivity to specific devices or websites. If the ping fails, it indicates a network issue.

4. **Check IP Address and DHCP:**

Ensure that devices have valid IP addresses assigned by the DHCP server.

5. **Flush DNS Cache:**

Clear the DNS cache on the computer to resolve DNS-related issues.

6. **Check Wi-Fi Signal Strength:**

If using Wi-Fi, check the signal strength to ensure a stable connection.

7. **Check Firewall and Security Software:**

Temporarily disable firewalls or security software to see if they are causing network connectivity problems.

8. **Check Router Settings:**

Review router settings for any misconfigurations that may affect network connectivity.

9. **Reset Router to Factory Settings:**

If the router is not functioning correctly, try resetting it to its factory settings and reconfiguring it.

10. **Scan for Malware:**

Malware can impact network performance. Run a thorough malware scan on all devices.

11. **Check Network Traffic and Bandwidth:**

Identify any devices or applications that might be using excessive bandwidth.

12. **Update Router Firmware:**

Ensure that the router firmware is up to date to fix known bugs and improve performance.

13. **Check Internet Service Provider (ISP) Status:**

Contact the ISP to check for any widespread network outages in your area.

14. **Check DNS Settings:**

Verify that DNS settings on the router or device are configured correctly to translate domain names to IP addresses.

15. Check Network Firewall and Security Settings:

Ensure that the network firewall or security settings are not blocking access to specific websites or services.

16. Use Network Troubleshooting Tools:

Utilize network troubleshooting tools like ipconfig (Windows) or ifconfig (Linux/macOS) to check network configurations and network interface status.

17. Check Router Firmware Compatibility:

Ensure that the router firmware is compatible with the devices and operating systems used in the network.

18. Update Network Drivers:

Update network drivers on computers and devices to fix compatibility issues and improve performance.

19. Test Network Connectivity on Different Devices:

Verify network connectivity on multiple devices to determine if the problem is isolated to a specific device or affects the entire network.

20. Check Bandwidth Usage:

Monitor bandwidth usage on the network to identify potential bandwidth hogs or excessive data consumption.

21. Perform a Traceroute:

Use the traceroute command to trace the path that packets take to reach a destination, helping to identify network bottlenecks.

22. Use Network Monitoring Software:

Implement network monitoring tools to track network performance and detect anomalies.

23. Check Wi-Fi Channel Interference:

Analyze Wi-Fi channel usage and switch to less crowded channels to improve wireless network performance.

24. **Reset Network Settings:**

If network issues persist, consider resetting network settings on devices and reconfiguring network connections.

25. **Contact Internet Service Provider (ISP):**

If the issue seems to be related to the internet connection, contact the ISP for further assistance and troubleshooting.

5.1 Troubleshooting Process and Tools

Effective troubleshooting involves a systematic approach to identify and resolve issues efficiently. Here's a general troubleshooting process and some commonly used tools for hardware, software, and network-related problems:

Troubleshooting Process:

1. **Identify the Problem:**

Start by gathering information about the issue, including specific error messages or symptoms.

Ask the user about recent changes or events that might have triggered the problem.

2. **Isolate the Cause:**

Determine if the problem is isolated to a specific device, software, or network.

Test other devices or connections to identify the scope of the issue.

3. **Research and Analyze:**

Use available resources, such as documentation, knowledge bases, or online forums, to research possible solutions.

Analyze system logs, event viewer, or error messages for additional insights.

4. **Create a Hypothesis:**

Based on the information gathered, formulate a hypothesis about the possible cause of the problem.

5. **Test the Hypothesis:**

Begin testing the most likely causes based on the hypothesis.

Test one variable at a time to determine the exact cause.

6. **Implement a Solution:**

Once the cause is identified, implement the appropriate solution or workaround.

7. **Verify and Test:**

After applying a solution, verify that the issue is resolved.

Test the system or network to ensure it is functioning as expected.

8. **Document the Solution:**

Document the troubleshooting steps taken and the final resolution for future reference.

Troubleshooting Tools:

1. **Diagnostic and System Utilities:**

Built-in diagnostic tools in operating systems, such as Windows Diagnostics, macOS Utilities, and Linux diagnostic commands.

2. **Task Manager and Activity Monitor:**

Monitor system performance, processes, and resource usage to identify resource-intensive applications or processes.

3. **Event Viewer:**

View system logs and error messages to identify critical events and pinpoint potential issues.

4. **Ping and Traceroute:**

Use the ping command to test network connectivity to a specific device or website.

Use the traceroute command to trace the path packets take to reach a destination.

5. **Network Monitoring Tools:**

Network monitoring software, like Wireshark, can capture and analyze network traffic to detect issues and anomalies.

6. **IPConfig and IFConfig:**

Use ipconfig (Windows) or ifconfig (Linux/macOS) to view and configure network settings.

7. **Wireless Signal Analysis Tools:**

Tools like NetSpot, inSSIDer, or Wi-Fi Analyzer can analyze Wi-Fi signal strength, interference, and channel usage.

8. **Hardware Diagnostic Tools:**

Many hardware components come with built-in diagnostic tools for testing their functionality.

9. **Ping Sweep and Port Scanning Tools:**

Use tools like Nmap to scan for active devices on a network and identify open ports.

10. **Remote Desktop Tools:**

Tools like TeamViewer or Remote Desktop Connection allow remote access to troubleshoot computers from a distance.

11. **System Restore (Windows) or Time Machine (macOS):**

These tools can revert the system to a previous state if issues are caused by recent changes.

12. **Antivirus and Malware Scanners:**

Use reputable antivirus software to scan and remove malware.

13. **Disk Cleanup and Disk Utility:**

Use Disk Cleanup (Windows) or Disk Utility (macOS) to optimize disk space and repair disk errors.

14. **Process Monitor:**

Monitor processes and applications in real-time to detect issues or resource conflicts.

5.2 Troubleshooting Motherboard, RAM, CPU, and Power

When troubleshooting issues related to the motherboard, RAM, CPU, and power components, it's essential to follow a structured approach. These components are critical for the proper functioning of a computer system, and problems with any of them can lead to various symptoms. Here are some troubleshooting steps for each component:

Motherboard:

1. **Visual Inspection:**

Perform a visual inspection of the motherboard for any visible signs of damage, such as burnt areas, bulging capacitors, or loose connections.

2. **Check Power Connections:**

Ensure that all power connectors to the motherboard are properly seated and secured.

3. **Remove Non-Essential Components:**

Temporarily remove all non-essential components (e.g., expansion cards, additional RAM) to check if the issue is related to conflicting hardware.

4. **Reset CMOS:**

Clear the CMOS settings by either using the motherboard's CMOS reset jumper or removing the CMOS battery for a few minutes.

5. **Inspect BIOS Settings:**

Check the BIOS settings for any misconfigurations or conflicting settings.

6. **Run Built-in Diagnostics:**

Many motherboards come with built-in diagnostic tools. Check the motherboard's manual for instructions on how to run diagnostics.

7. **Test with a Known-Good Power Supply:**

If possible, test the motherboard with a known-good power supply to rule out power-related issues.

RAM:

1. **Reseat RAM Modules:**

Remove and reseat all RAM modules to ensure they are properly inserted into their slots.

2. **Test Each RAM Module Individually:**

Test each RAM module individually by booting the system with only one module installed at a time. This helps identify faulty RAM.

3. **Swap RAM Slots:**

If the motherboard has multiple RAM slots, try swapping the RAM modules to check if a specific slot is causing the issue.

4. **Run Memory Diagnostics:**

Use built-in memory diagnostics tools like Windows Memory Diagnostic or third-party tools like

Memtest86 to test the RAM for errors.

5. **Check RAM Compatibility:**

Verify that the RAM is compatible with the motherboard and meets the required specifications.

CPU:

1. **Check CPU Connections:**

Ensure that the CPU is properly seated in its socket, and the CPU cooler is securely attached.

2. **Inspect for Physical Damage:**

Check the CPU for any physical damage, bent pins, or burn marks.

3. **Monitor CPU Temperature:**

Use software tools like Core Temp or HWMonitor to monitor CPU temperature for overheating issues.

4. **Test with a Known-Good CPU:**

If possible, test the motherboard with a known-good CPU to rule out CPU-related problems.

Power Components:

1. **Check Power Supply Unit (PSU):**

Test the PSU using a PSU tester or replace it with a known-good PSU to verify if it's functioning correctly.

2. **Test Power Cables and Connectors:**

Check all power cables and connectors for damage or loose connections.

3. **Check Power Switch and Buttons:**

Verify that the power switch and other buttons on the case are working correctly.

4. **Verify Power Outlet and Surge Protection:**

Test the power outlet with other devices or use a surge protector to prevent power fluctuations.

5. **Use a Power Supply Tester:**

If available, use a power supply tester to check the voltage levels and stability of the PSU.

5.3 Troubleshooting Hard Drives and RAID Arrays

Troubleshooting issues with hard drives and RAID arrays is crucial for maintaining data integrity and preventing data loss. Here are some steps and tools to help troubleshoot problems related to hard drives and RAID configurations:

Troubleshooting Hard Drives:

1. **Check Drive Connections:**

Ensure that all data and power cables connecting the hard drive to the motherboard and power supply are secure.

2. **Listen for Unusual Sounds:**

Listen for clicking, grinding, or unusual sounds coming from the hard drive, as they could indicate a hardware failure.

3. **Use SMART Monitoring:**

SMART (Self-Monitoring, Analysis, and Reporting Technology) provides information about a hard drive's health. Use tools like CrystalDiskInfo (Windows) or smartctl (Linux/macOS) to check SMART status.

4. **Check Disk Management (Windows) or Disk Utility (macOS):**

Use Disk Management (Windows) or Disk Utility (macOS) to verify if the hard drive is recognized and properly formatted.

5. **Run Disk Check:**

Use CHKDSK (Windows) or fsck (Linux/macOS) to check and repair file system errors on the hard drive.

6. **Check for Bad Sectors:**

Use tools like HD Tune (Windows) or badblocks (Linux) to scan for bad sectors on the hard drive.

7. **Update Hard Drive Firmware:**

Check the manufacturer's website for firmware updates that could resolve known issues.

8. **Perform Data Backup:**

If data is accessible, back up important files immediately to prevent potential data loss during troubleshooting.

Troubleshooting RAID Arrays:

1. **Check RAID Controller Status:**

Ensure the RAID controller is functioning correctly and that no errors are reported during the boot process.

2. **Inspect Drive Connections:**

Verify that all drives in the RAID array are securely connected to the RAID controller and power supply.

3. **Check RAID Array Status:**

Use RAID management software to check the status of the RAID array and the health of individual drives.

4. **Rebuild RAID Array:**

If a drive fails in a RAID array, follow the appropriate steps to rebuild the array using a replacement drive.

5. **Replace Failed Drives:**

If a drive in the RAID array has failed, replace it with a new drive of the same size and type.

6. **Check RAID Configuration:**

Verify that the RAID configuration (RAID 0, RAID 1, RAID 5, etc.) is set correctly in the RAID controller BIOS or software.

7. **Update RAID Controller Firmware:**

Check the RAID controller manufacturer's website for firmware updates that could address RAID-related issues.

8. **Monitor RAID Alerts:**

Configure RAID monitoring software to send alerts when issues with the array or individual drives are detected.

RAID Recovery and Data Loss:

If you encounter severe issues with a RAID array, such as multiple drive failures, it may be necessary to contact a data recovery specialist for professional assistance. Attempting to rebuild the array in such cases could lead to data loss or corruption.

Before performing any significant changes to RAID configurations or hard drives, ensure you have a verified backup of your important data. RAID arrays are not a substitute for regular data backups.

Remember that RAID is not a substitute for backups, and data should be backed up regularly to a separate storage solution. RAID offers improved performance, fault tolerance, and increased storage capacity, but it does not protect against data loss due to other factors like accidental deletions, viruses, or hardware failures beyond RAID's capabilities.

As with any troubleshooting, exercise caution, and if you are unsure about any steps, consider seeking assistance from an experienced IT professional or RAID specialist.

5.4 Troubleshooting Network Issues

Network issues can disrupt communication, access to resources, and internet connectivity. Troubleshooting network problems involves a methodical approach to identify and resolve the root causes. Here are some steps to troubleshoot common network issues:

1. Check Physical Connections:

Ensure all network cables are securely connected to devices and network ports. Check for any damaged or loose cables.

2. Verify Power and Connectivity of Networking Devices:

Check that network switches, routers, and modems have power and indicator lights indicating connectivity.

3. Restart Networking Devices:

Power cycle networking devices (router, modem, switches) to refresh connections and resolve temporary issues.

4. Check IP Configuration:

Verify that devices have valid IP addresses assigned through DHCP or are properly configured with static IPs where required.

5. Test Connectivity to Gateway/Router:

Ping the default gateway or router IP address to check if the device can reach the local network.

6. Run Network Troubleshooting Tools:

Use built-in network troubleshooting tools like ipconfig (Windows), ifconfig (Linux/macOS), or Network Diagnostics (macOS) to diagnose and repair network issues.

7. Ping External Resources:

Ping external websites or DNS servers (e.g., 8.8.8.8) to determine if there's connectivity to the internet.

8. Check DNS Settings:

Verify DNS settings on devices to ensure they can resolve domain names to IP addresses.

9. Scan for Malware:

Perform malware scans on devices to check for any malicious software affecting network performance.

10. Check Firewall Settings

Verify that firewall settings are not blocking necessary network traffic.

11. Check Wi-Fi Signal Strength:

For Wi-Fi networks, check the signal strength to ensure a stable connection.

12. Update Network Drivers:

Update network drivers on computers to resolve compatibility issues and improve performance.

13. Restart Network Services:

Restart network-related services (e.g., DHCP, DNS) to refresh configurations.

14. Check for Bandwidth Usage:

Identify devices or applications that might be consuming excessive bandwidth.

15. Review Event Logs:

Check event logs on devices for network-related errors or warnings.

16. Disable and Re-enable Network Adapter:

Temporarily disable and re-enable the network adapter on the device to reset the connection.

17. Use Traceroute:

Use traceroute to trace the path of network packets to a destination and identify network bottlenecks.

18. Monitor Network Traffic:

Use network monitoring tools like Wireshark to capture and analyze network traffic for anomalies.

19. Reset Network Settings:

If issues persist, consider resetting network settings on devices and reconfiguring network connections.

20. Check Network Switches and Hubs:

Inspect network switches and hubs for connectivity issues, port errors, or indicator light abnormalities.

21. Test Connectivity to Specific IP Addresses:

Ping specific IP addresses (e.g., network servers) to determine if there are issues accessing particular resources.

22. Use Network Diagnostic Commands:

Utilize network diagnostic commands like nslookup (Windows, Linux) or dig (Linux) to troubleshoot DNS resolution issues.

23. Review Router Configuration:

Check router configurations for any misconfigurations or access restrictions that might affect network connectivity.

24. Look for IP Address Conflicts:

Verify that there are no IP address conflicts on the network, as they can cause connectivity problems.

25. Check Wireless Frequency and Channels:

For Wi-Fi networks, ensure the wireless frequency (2.4GHz or 5GHz) and channels are optimal to avoid interference.

26. Use Network Troubleshooting Wizards:

Some operating systems have built-in network troubleshooting wizards that can automatically diagnose and fix common network issues.

27. Check Network Security Settings:

Ensure that security settings (e.g., WPA/WPA2 passwords, firewall rules) are configured correctly to allow legitimate access.

28. Check for Network Congestion:

Monitor network traffic during peak hours to identify potential congestion points that could lead to slow connections.

29. Check Network Cables for Damage:

Inspect network cables for physical damage, as damaged cables can cause intermittent connectivity issues.

30. Test Network Connectivity with Other Devices:

Check network connectivity with different devices to determine if the issue is specific to one device or affects multiple devices.

31. Update Router Firmware:

Ensure the router's firmware is up to date to fix known issues and improve performance.

32. Check Quality of Service (QoS) Settings:

Adjust QoS settings on the router to prioritize network traffic for essential services or devices.

33. Use Wi-Fi Analyzer Tools:

Utilize Wi-Fi analyzer tools to identify Wi-Fi signal strength, channel congestion, and potential interference sources.

34. Verify VLAN Configurations:

If your network uses VLANs (Virtual LANs), check VLAN configurations to ensure correct segmentation and access controls.

35. Check Network Access Control Lists (ACLs):

Review network ACLs to confirm they are not inadvertently blocking legitimate traffic.

36. Reboot Network Devices:

In some cases, a simple reboot of routers, switches, and access points can resolve temporary network issues.

37. Check ISP Status and Outages:

If experiencing internet connectivity problems, check with your Internet Service Provider (ISP) to see if there are any service outages in your area.

Quiz

1. Which component is often referred to as the "brain" of the computer?
   a) Motherboard
   b) CPU (Central Processing Unit)
   c) RAM (Random Access Memory)
   d) Hard Drive

2. What is the primary function of the BIOS (Basic Input/Output System) in a computer?
   a) Display graphics on the screen
   b) Manage input devices like keyboard and mouse
   c) Initialize hardware and start the operating system
   d) Store user data and files

3. Which of the following is a type of non-volatile memory that retains data even when the power is off?
   a) RAM (Random Access Memory)
   b) CPU Cache
   c) SSD (Solid State Drive)
   d) HDD (Hard Disk Drive)

4. What is the purpose of the GPU (Graphics Processing Unit) in a computer?
   a) To process mathematical calculations
   b) To control the flow of data between different components
   c) To display graphics and images on the screen
   d) To manage network connections

5. Which component is responsible for storing the operating system, software applications, and user data in a computer?
   a) RAM (Random Access Memory)
   b) CPU (Central Processing Unit)
   c) Motherboard
   d) Storage Device (e.g., HDD or SSD)

6. What type of port is commonly used to connect a printer to a computer?
   a) USB (Universal Serial Bus)
   b) HDMI (High-Definition Multimedia Interface)
   c) Ethernet
   d) VGA (Video Graphics Array)

7. The acronym "LAN" stands for:
   a) Local Access Network
   b) Local Area Network
   c) Long Access Network
   d) Long Area Network

8. Which device is used to connect multiple network devices together and facilitate data communication within a network?
   a) Modem
   b) Router
   c) Switch
   d) Hub

9. Which network topology connects all devices to a single central hub or switch?
   a) Bus Topology
   b) Ring Topology
   c) Star Topology
   d) Mesh Topology

10. Which networking protocol is commonly used for secure data transmission over the internet?
    a) HTTP (Hypertext Transfer Protocol)
    b) FTP (File Transfer Protocol)
    c) SMTP (Simple Mail Transfer Protocol)
    d) HTTPS (Hypertext Transfer Protocol Secure)

11. What is the first step in the troubleshooting process?
    a) Implement a solution
    b) Identify the problem
    c) Create a hypothesis
    d) Test the hypothesis

12. What tool can be used to analyze network traffic and detect anomalies?
    a) Wireshark
    b) Task Manager
    c) Disk Cleanup
    d) Event Viewer

13. What is the purpose of running the "chkdsk" command in Windows?
    a) Check and repair file system errors on the hard drive

b) Monitor CPU performance

c) Test network connectivity

d) Check disk space usage

14. When troubleshooting network connectivity issues, which command can be used to test if a device can reach the default gateway or router?

a) ping

b) tracert

c) ipconfig

d) netstat

15. What should you do first when troubleshooting a hardware issue on a computer?

a) Update device drivers

b) Perform a system restore

c) Check physical connections and power

d) Run a disk cleanup

16. Which network troubleshooting command allows you to view the IP configuration of a device?

a) ipconfig (Windows) / ifconfig (Linux, macOS)

b) ping

c) traceroute (tracert on Windows)

d) nslookup

17. When troubleshooting a network issue, which step involves testing different possible causes one at a time?

a) Identify the problem

b) Create a hypothesis

c) Implement a solution

d) Test the hypothesis

18. What type of software tools are used to capture and analyze network packets for troubleshooting purposes?

a) Antivirus software

b) Network monitoring tools

c) Disk cleanup tools

d) Registry cleaners

19. What does the acronym "RAID" stand for in data storage configurations?

a) Redundant Array of Inexpensive Disks

b) Random Access Interconnected Devices

c) Reliable Array of Independent Disks

d) Remote Access Intranet Devices

20. Which RAID level offers both data redundancy and improved read and write performance?

a) RAID 0

b) RAID 1

c) RAID 5

d) RAID 10

21. What type of operating system is commonly used on smartphones and tablets?

a) Windows

b) macOS

c) Linux

d) Android (or iOS)

22. Which of the following is an example of a mobile operating system developed by Apple?

a) Android

b) iOS

c) Windows Mobile

d) Ubuntu Touch

23. What does the term "App" stand for in the context of mobile devices?

a) Application

b) Applet

c) Applicable

d) Apprehensive

24. Which feature allows users to unlock their smartphones using their fingerprint?

a) Face ID

b) Touch ID

c) Face Unlock

d) Fingerprint Scanner

25. What does the term "4G" refer to in mobile communication technology?

a) The fourth generation of mobile operating systems

b) The fourth generation of smartphones

c) The fourth generation of mobile networks

d) The fourth generation of mobile apps

26. What does the term "4G" refer to in mobile communication technology?
    a) The fourth generation of mobile operating systems
    b) The fourth generation of smartphones
    c) The fourth generation of mobile networks
    d) The fourth generation of mobile apps

27. Which mobile communication technology provides higher data speeds and better network performance compared to 4G?
    a) 3G
    b) 4G
    c) 5G
    d) 2G

28. What is the process of downloading and installing updates for a mobile operating system called?
    a) Rooting
    b) Flashing
    c) Updating
    d) Jailbreaking

29. Which mobile device feature allows users to determine their device's geographical location?
    a) GPS (Global Positioning System)
    b) NFC (Near Field Communication)
    c) Bluetooth
    d) Accelerometer

30. **Networking Protocols and Services:**

31. Which protocol is used to send and receive emails on the internet?
    a) HTTP (Hypertext Transfer Protocol)
    b) FTP (File Transfer Protocol)
    c) SMTP (Simple Mail Transfer Protocol)
    d) HTTPS (Hypertext Transfer Protocol Secure)

32. Which protocol is responsible for converting domain names (e.g., www.example.com) to IP addresses?
    a) DHCP (Dynamic Host Configuration Protocol)
    b) DNS (Domain Name System)
    c) ICMP (Internet Control Message Protocol)

d) NAT (Network Address Translation)

33. What tool can be used to analyze network traffic and detect anomalies?

    a) Wireshark

    b) Task Manager

    c) Disk Cleanup

    d) Event Viewer

34. What is the purpose of running the "chkdsk" command in Windows?

    a) Check and repair file system errors on the hard drive

    b) Monitor CPU performance

    c) Test network connectivity

    d) Check disk space usage

35. When troubleshooting network connectivity issues, which command can be used to test if a device can reach the default gateway or router?

    a) ping

    b) tracert

    c) ipconfig

    d) netstat

36. What should you do first when troubleshooting a hardware issue on a computer?

    a) Update device drivers

    b) Perform a system restore

    c) Check physical connections and power

    d) Run a disk cleanup

37. Which network troubleshooting command allows you to view the IP configuration of a device?

    a) ipconfig (Windows) / ifconfig (Linux, macOS)

    b) ping

    c) traceroute (tracert on Windows)

    d) nslookup

38. What type of operating system is commonly used on smartphones and tablets?

    a) Windows

    b) macOS

    c) Linux

    d) Android (or iOS)

39. Which of the following is an example of a mobile operating system developed by Apple?

a) Android

b) iOS

c) Windows Mobile

d) Ubuntu Touch

40. What does the term "App" stand for in the context of mobile devices?

a) Application

b) Applet

c) Applicable

d) Apprehensive

41. Which feature allows users to unlock their smartphones using their fingerprint?

a) Face ID

b) Touch ID

c) Face Unlock

d) Fingerprint Scanner

42. What does the term "4G" refer to in mobile communication technology?

a) The fourth generation of mobile operating systems

b) The fourth generation of smartphones

c) The fourth generation of mobile networks

d) The fourth generation of mobile apps

Operating Systems

An operating system (OS) is a fundamental software that manages computer hardware and software resources and provides services to enable applications to run and interact with the computer. It acts as an intermediary between the hardware and software, making it easier for users and applications to interact with the computer system. Let's explore the key concepts related to operating systems:

1. Types of Operating Systems:

- **Single-User, Single-Tasking OS:** Supports one user and allows only one application to run at a time (e.g., MS-DOS).
- **Single-User, Multi-Tasking OS:** Supports one user but allows multiple applications to run simultaneously (e.g., Windows, macOS, Linux).
- **Multi-User OS:** Supports multiple users, allowing each user to run multiple applications concurrently (e.g., UNIX, Linux server editions).
- **Real-Time OS:** Designed for time-critical applications, where response times are critical (e.g., industrial control systems).
- **Embedded OS:** Optimized for specific devices or systems (e.g., Android for smartphones, RTOS for microcontrollers).

2. Functions of an Operating System:

- **Process Management:** Manages processes (running programs) by allocating CPU time, creating and terminating processes, and handling inter-process communication.
- **Memory Management:** Allocates and manages memory space for processes and data, ensuring efficient utilization of RAM.
- **File System Management:** Manages file storage, organization, and access for user data and applications.
- **Device Management:** Controls and coordinates interaction with hardware devices such as printers, keyboards, and disk drives.
- **User Interface:** Provides a graphical or command-line interface through which users interact with the computer.

3. Process Scheduling Algorithms:

- **First-Come, First-Served (FCFS):** Schedules processes in the order they arrive. Simple but may cause longer wait times for short processes.

- **Shortest Job Next (SJN):** Prioritizes the shortest jobs first, reducing average waiting times. Not practical for real-time systems.
- **Round Robin (RR):** Allocates a fixed time slice to each process, allowing fair CPU time sharing among processes.
- **Priority Scheduling:** Assigns priority levels to processes, and higher-priority processes are executed before lower-priority ones.

4. Memory Management Techniques:

- **Fixed Partitioning:** Memory is divided into fixed-sized partitions, and processes are assigned to these partitions.
- **Dynamic Partitioning:** Memory is divided into variable-sized partitions to accommodate varying process sizes.
- **Paging:** Divides memory and processes into fixed-sized pages, allowing non-contiguous allocation.
- **Segmentation:** Divides processes into logical segments of varying sizes, providing better memory utilization.

5. File Systems:

- **FAT (File Allocation Table):** Simple file system used in older Windows versions, limited in features.
- **NTFS (New Technology File System):** Advanced file system used in modern Windows versions, offering better security and performance.
- **Ext4:** Commonly used in Linux systems, offering improved performance and reliability over its predecessors.
- **HFS+ (Mac OS Extended):** File system used in macOS systems, supporting larger file sizes and journaling.

6. Virtualization:

- **Virtual Machines (VMs):** Allows multiple operating systems to run on a single physical machine simultaneously.
- **Containers:** Isolates applications and their dependencies to improve portability and scalability.

7. Troubleshooting Operating System Issues:

- **Blue Screen of Death (BSOD):** Common in Windows systems, caused by critical system errors.

- **Kernel Panics:** Common in macOS and Linux systems, caused by serious kernel-level errors.
- **Freezing or Hanging:** When the system becomes unresponsive, often due to resource contention or hardware issues.
- **Application Crashes:** Caused by software bugs or compatibility issues.
- **Slow Performance:** Can be due to insufficient resources, background processes, or malware.

8. File and Directory Permissions:

File Permissions: Operating systems implement access control to protect files from unauthorized access. Permissions are typically represented as read (r), write (w), and execute (x) for the owner, group, and others. For example, "rw-r--r--" means the owner can read and write the file, while others can only read it.

Directory Permissions: Directories also have permissions, but the execute (x) permission is required to access the contents of a directory. Without execute permission, users cannot list the files within the directory.

9. Boot Process:

BIOS/UEFI: The Basic Input/Output System (BIOS) or Unified Extensible Firmware Interface (UEFI) initializes hardware and locates the boot loader.

Boot Loader: The boot loader (e.g., GRUB in Linux or NTLDR in Windows) loads the operating system kernel into memory.

Kernel: The kernel is loaded into memory and takes control of the boot process. It initializes device drivers, mounts the root file system, and starts the init process.

Init Process: The init process (or systemd in modern Linux distributions) is the first user-space process and initializes the rest of the system, including starting essential services.

10. Process States:

Running: The process is currently using the CPU.

Ready: The process is waiting to be assigned the CPU and is ready to run.

Blocked (or Waiting): The process is waiting for some event to occur (e.g., I/O completion) before it can continue.

11. Virtual Memory:

Virtual Memory allows the OS to use a portion of the hard drive as an extension of RAM. This enables running more programs than the physical RAM can accommodate.

When a process needs more memory than available physical RAM, the OS moves less frequently used parts of memory to the disk, freeing up space for active processes.

12. Task Manager (Windows) and Activity Monitor (macOS):

Task Manager (Windows) and Activity Monitor (macOS) are tools that display information about running processes, memory usage, CPU usage, and disk activity.

Users and administrators can use these tools to monitor the system's performance, identify resource-intensive processes, and terminate or troubleshoot misbehaving applications.

13. System Updates and Patch Management:

Operating systems regularly receive updates and patches to fix bugs, enhance security, and improve performance.

Users should regularly update their systems to protect against security vulnerabilities and ensure optimal functionality.

14. System Restore and Recovery:

System Restore (Windows) and Time Machine (macOS) are tools that allow users to revert the system to a previous state, helping to recover from system malfunctions or software-related issues.

Backup solutions like Time Machine (macOS) and File History (Windows) enable users to restore lost or corrupted files.

15. Graphical User Interface (GUI):

GUI provides a visual and interactive way for users to interact with the computer using windows, icons, menus, and pointers (WIMP).

Popular GUIs include the Windows Desktop environment, macOS's Aqua, and various Linux desktop environments like GNOME and KDE.

16. Command-Line Interface (CLI):

CLI allows users to interact with the computer using text-based commands, typically through a terminal or command prompt.

CLI is commonly used in scripting, automation, and advanced system administration tasks.

17. Mobile Operating System Features:

Mobile OSes focus on touch-based interfaces, portability, and power efficiency.

Features include app stores, gesture-based navigation, battery optimization, mobile-specific security measures, and synchronization with cloud services.

6.1 Windows OS

Windows OS, developed by Microsoft, is one of the most widely used operating systems in the world. It is known for its user-friendly interface, extensive software compatibility, and broad hardware support. Throughout its history, Microsoft has released various versions of Windows, each with its features and improvements. Here are some key aspects of Windows OS:

1. Windows Versions:

- **Windows 3.1/3.11:** Early versions with a graphical user interface (GUI), but still heavily reliant on MS-DOS.
- **Windows 95/98/ME:** Introduced the Start menu, taskbar, and plug-and-play support for hardware.
- **Windows NT/2000:** Aimed at business users with advanced security features and better stability.
- **Windows XP:** A popular and long-lasting version, known for its stability and user-friendly interface.
- **Windows Vista:** Introduced Aero visual style but faced criticism for its performance and compatibility issues.
- **Windows 7:** A significant improvement over Vista, offering better performance and user experience.
- **Windows 8/8.1:** Introduced a touch-oriented interface, but received mixed reactions from users.
- **Windows 10:** The latest version, known for combining features from Windows 7 and 8, with regular updates and improvements.

2. User Interface:

Windows OS features a graphical user interface (GUI) with a Start menu, taskbar, and desktop environment.

Users can customize the desktop with icons, shortcuts, and widgets.

3. File Explorer:

File Explorer (formerly Windows Explorer) is used to browse and manage files and folders.

It provides access to drives, libraries, and network locations.

4. System Updates:

Windows OS receives regular updates and patches to improve security, stability, and functionality.

Windows Update automatically delivers these updates to users.

5. Windows Defender:

Windows OS includes Windows Defender, a built-in antivirus and anti-malware solution.

It provides real-time protection against viruses and other threats.

6. Virtual Desktops:

Windows 10 introduced the ability to create and manage multiple virtual desktops for better organization and multitasking.

7. Cortana:

Cortana is a digital assistant available on Windows 10 that can answer questions, set reminders, and perform tasks.

8. DirectX and Gaming Support:

Windows is a preferred OS for gaming due to its support for DirectX, a collection of APIs for handling multimedia tasks, including graphics rendering.

9. BitLocker:

BitLocker is a full-disk encryption feature in some Windows editions to protect data from unauthorized access.

10. Windows Store:

The Windows Store (now Microsoft Store) offers a wide range of applications and games for download and installation.

11. Windows Subsystem for Linux (WSL):

WSL allows users to run a Linux environment within Windows, enabling the use of Linux command-line tools and utilities.

12. Remote Desktop:

Windows OS provides the Remote Desktop feature, allowing users to access and control their desktop remotely from another device.

13. Windows Editions:

Windows OS comes in different editions tailored for various user needs and environments. Some common editions include Windows Home, Windows Pro, Windows Enterprise, and Windows Education.

Windows Home: Designed for home users and includes essential features like Cortana, Windows Defender, and Windows Update.

Windows Pro: Targeted at small businesses and advanced users, it includes additional features like BitLocker, Remote Desktop, and Group Policy management.

Windows Enterprise: Aimed at large organizations, it includes advanced security and management features like Windows Update for Business and AppLocker.

Windows Education: Optimized for educational institutions, it provides features like Group Policy for schools and universities.

14. Windows Compatibility:

Windows OS is known for its broad hardware and software compatibility. It supports a wide range of devices, including desktops, laptops, tablets, and 2-in-1 devices.

Many software applications, including productivity tools, games, and multimedia software, are developed to run on Windows, making it a popular choice for users and businesses.

15. Windows Activation:

Windows OS requires activation to verify that it is a genuine copy of the operating system.

Activation can be done online or by phone, and it is required for continued use beyond a trial period or for certain features to function correctly.

16. Windows Troubleshooting:

Windows OS provides built-in troubleshooting tools and diagnostic utilities to help users identify and resolve various issues.

The Windows Event Viewer allows users to view system events and logs to pinpoint problems.

Windows Reliability Monitor provides a timeline of system events and errors to assess system stability.

17. Windows System Restore:

Windows System Restore allows users to roll back the system to a previous state in case of software-related issues.

It creates restore points before installing new software or system updates, allowing users to undo changes if necessary.

18. Windows Safe Mode:

Safe Mode is a diagnostic mode in Windows that loads only essential drivers and services, allowing users to troubleshoot issues caused by third-party software or drivers.

19. Windows Backup and Restore:

Windows OS includes backup and restore utilities to back up important files and restore them in case of data loss.

Users can set up automated backups to an external drive or network location.

20. Windows Disk Cleanup:

Disk Cleanup is a tool to free up disk space by removing unnecessary files, temporary files, and system files that are no longer needed.

21. Windows Task Manager:

Windows Task Manager allows users to monitor and manage running processes, performance, and startup programs.

It is a valuable tool for troubleshooting and identifying resource-intensive processes.

22. Windows Command Prompt and PowerShell:

Windows OS provides both Command Prompt (CMD) and PowerShell for command-line operations and system administration tasks.

PowerShell offers more advanced features and scripting capabilities for managing Windows systems.

23. Windows Remote Assistance:

Windows Remote Assistance enables users to request or offer remote technical assistance from other Windows users.

It allows a trusted person to remotely view or control the desktop to assist with troubleshooting.

24. Windows Security Features:

Windows OS includes various security features like Windows Defender Antivirus, Windows Firewall, User Account Control (UAC), and Secure Boot.

Windows Security Center provides a centralized interface to manage security settings.

6.2 Other Operating Systems (Linux, Mac OS)

In addition to Windows, there are other popular operating systems used by individuals and organizations. These include Linux and macOS, each with its unique features and strengths:

1. Linux:

Linux is an open-source operating system based on the Linux kernel, developed collaboratively by a community of developers worldwide.

Linux comes in various distributions (distros), such as Ubuntu, Fedora, CentOS, Debian, and more. Each distro may have specific use cases and target audiences.

Linux is highly customizable and modular, allowing users to choose from various desktop environments (e.g., GNOME, KDE, XFCE) and package managers (e.g., APT, DNF, Pacman).

Linux is known for its stability, security, and performance, making it a popular choice for servers and supercomputers.

Linux supports a wide range of hardware and architectures, making it adaptable to different devices and embedded systems.

Linux is the preferred OS for developers, providing robust command-line tools and a vast software repository.

Linux has a strong focus on security, with regular updates and patches to address vulnerabilities.

Linux can be used as a desktop OS, server OS, or embedded OS, and it powers many devices, including Android smartphones.

2. macOS:

macOS is the operating system developed by Apple Inc. for its Macintosh computers.

macOS is known for its intuitive user interface, design aesthetics, and seamless integration with Apple's ecosystem.

macOS offers features like Time Machine (backup), iCloud synchronization, and Continuity (seamless integration with iOS devices).

macOS includes a UNIX-based architecture, making it a powerful OS for developers and programmers.

macOS is optimized for performance and battery efficiency on Apple's hardware.

macOS comes with built-in security features, including Gatekeeper (application verification), FileVault (disk encryption), and XProtect (malware protection).

macOS supports virtualization through technologies like Boot Camp and Parallels Desktop, enabling users to run Windows and Linux alongside macOS.

macOS is widely used in creative industries for video editing, graphic design, and music production due to its robust multimedia capabilities.

3. Linux Desktop Environments:

Linux offers a variety of desktop environments, each providing a different look and feel to the user interface.

GNOME: A modern and user-friendly desktop environment known for its simplicity and elegance.

KDE Plasma: A feature-rich and customizable desktop environment with a visually appealing interface.

XFCE: A lightweight and fast desktop environment, suitable for older hardware and systems with limited resources.

Cinnamon: A user-friendly desktop environment that provides a familiar interface for Windows users transitioning to Linux.

Mate: A fork of the classic GNOME 2 desktop environment, offering a traditional and straightforward interface.

4. Package Management:

Linux uses package managers to install, update, and remove software packages from a central repository.

Common package managers include APT (Advanced Package Tool) for Debian-based distros, DNF (Dandified Yum) for Fedora-based distros, and Pacman for Arch-based distros.

Package managers simplify software management, resolving dependencies and handling updates efficiently.

5. Command-Line Interface (CLI):

Linux is renowned for its powerful command-line interface (CLI), offering a wide range of commands and tools for system administration, scripting, and automation.

Users can perform various tasks using the terminal, making Linux an ideal choice for developers and advanced users.

6. macOS Features:

macOS boasts a sleek and intuitive user interface with a focus on aesthetics and ease of use.

Continuity: Seamlessly integrates macOS with iOS devices, allowing users to make and receive phone calls, send messages, and share files across devices.

Time Machine: Provides automatic and reliable backup to an external storage device, ensuring data recovery in case of system failure.

Spotlight Search: An efficient search tool that quickly locates files, applications, and information on the system.

iCloud: Syncs files, photos, calendars, and other data across all Apple devices.

Launchpad: A quick way to access and organize applications in a grid layout, similar to iOS.

7. Terminal (macOS):

macOS offers a UNIX-based terminal with a vast array of command-line utilities and tools.

Developers and power users often leverage the terminal for tasks such as scripting, version control, and system configuration.

8. Security and Privacy (macOS):

macOS includes built-in security features like Gatekeeper, which verifies the authenticity of downloaded applications to prevent malware.

FileVault provides disk encryption to protect sensitive data from unauthorized access.

macOS emphasizes user privacy, offering users more control over app permissions and data sharing.

9. Integration with Apple Ecosystem:

macOS is tightly integrated with other Apple devices and services, allowing seamless synchronization of data through iCloud.

Handoff enables users to start a task on one device and continue it on another, like composing an email on an iPhone and finishing it on a Mac.

10. Software Availability:

While macOS has a broad range of applications available, it may have fewer options compared to Windows.

However, the macOS App Store and third-party developers offer numerous software choices for productivity, creative work, and entertainment.

6.3 Software Installation, Configuration, and Management

Installing, configuring, and managing software is a fundamental aspect of using any operating system. Users and system administrators need to be familiar with these processes to efficiently set up and maintain their systems. Let's explore the key aspects of software installation, configuration, and management:

1. Software Installation:

Windows: In Windows, software installation is usually done through executable files with the extension ".exe" or installer packages with ".msi" extensions. Users can download software from the internet or install it from physical media (CD/DVD). Many applications also come from the Microsoft Store.

Linux: Linux uses package managers to install software from official repositories or third-party sources. Package managers handle dependencies and ensure that software is correctly installed. Popular package managers include APT (Debian/Ubuntu), DNF/YUM (Fedora/RHEL), and Pacman (Arch Linux).

macOS: On macOS, users typically install applications from DMG (Disk Image) files. Users mount the DMG file and drag the application to the Applications folder. Some applications come with their own installers or use package managers like Homebrew.

2. Software Configuration:

Windows: After installing software on Windows, users often need to configure settings through the application's built-in preferences or settings menu.

Linux: Linux applications usually store configuration files in the user's home directory. Users can modify these text-based configuration files using text editors to customize the behavior of applications.

macOS: macOS applications generally store configuration files in the user's Library folder. Users can access and edit these settings using the application's preferences.

3. Software Updates and Patches:

Windows: Windows OS provides regular updates through Windows Update, which includes security patches, bug fixes, and feature updates.

Linux: Linux distributions offer updates through package managers. Users can regularly run "update" and "upgrade" commands to keep the system and applications up to date.

macOS: macOS provides updates and security patches through the App Store and system updates. Users should regularly check for updates and apply them.

4. Software Uninstallation:

Windows: Uninstalling software in Windows can be done through the Control Panel or the "Add or Remove Programs" (older versions) or "Programs and Features" (newer versions) option.

Linux: Linux users can uninstall software using the package manager. For example, on Ubuntu, users can run "sudo apt remove <package-name>" in the terminal.

macOS: macOS users can uninstall applications by dragging them from the Applications folder to the Trash. Some applications may come with uninstaller scripts.

5. Software Repositories and App Stores:

Linux: Linux distributions maintain official software repositories, which contain a wide range of applications. Users can use package managers to install software from these repositories. Some distributions also have third-party repositories and community-contributed packages.

macOS: macOS has the App Store, which provides a curated selection of applications. Users can also download and install software from various websites or use third-party package managers like Homebrew.

6. Software Licensing:

Users must respect software licensing terms and conditions when installing and using applications.

Some software is open source and freely available, while others are commercial products with different licensing models.

Users should review and comply with licensing agreements to ensure legal and ethical use of the software.

7. Software Dependencies:

Windows: Windows applications may have dependencies on certain system libraries or runtime components called DLLs (Dynamic Link Libraries). These dependencies are often bundled with the application installer or installed separately as redistributable packages.

Linux: Linux package managers handle dependencies automatically, ensuring that all required libraries and components are installed when installing software. This simplifies the installation process and avoids compatibility issues.

macOS: macOS applications may also have dependencies on system libraries or frameworks. macOS package managers like Homebrew manage dependencies and install required components when installing software.

8. Software Virtualization and Containers:

Virtualization allows users to run multiple operating systems or software instances on a single physical machine. Virtualization software like VMware and VirtualBox creates virtual machines (VMs) to host other operating systems.

Containers, such as Docker, provide a lightweight alternative to virtualization. Containers isolate applications and their dependencies, enabling easy deployment and portability across different environments.

9. Software Repositories and Package Sources:

Linux distributions have official repositories maintained by the distribution's community. Users can also add third-party repositories or personal package archives (PPAs) to access additional software.

macOS users can access the App Store for applications vetted by Apple. For additional software, users can download directly from developers' websites or use package managers like Homebrew.

10. Software Installation from Source Code:

In addition to using package managers, Linux users can install software from source code. This involves downloading the application's source files, compiling them, and installing the resulting binary.

Installing from source allows users to customize build options and access the latest features, but it can be more complex than using package managers.

11. Software Configuration Management Tools:

For system administrators managing multiple machines, configuration management tools like Ansible, Puppet, and Chef automate software installation, configuration, and updates across a network of computers.

These tools ensure consistency and reduce manual intervention, making it easier to manage large-scale software deployments.

12. Software Licensing Management:

In organizations, software licensing management is crucial to ensure compliance with licensing agreements and prevent unauthorized use of software.

IT administrators need to track licenses, monitor software usage, and ensure that the right number of licenses is purchased for each application.

13. Software Backup and Recovery:

Regularly backing up software configurations and settings is essential for disaster recovery and system migration.

Backup solutions like Time Machine (macOS), File History (Windows), and third-party tools on Linux help users restore their software configurations in case of system failure.

14. Application Performance Monitoring (APM):

For businesses and large-scale software deployments, APM tools monitor application performance, track resource usage, and detect potential bottlenecks or issues.

APM tools help optimize application performance and ensure smooth user experiences.

Quiz

1. What is the role of an operating system?
    a) Manage hardware resources
    b) Manage software applications
    c) Provide a user-friendly interface
    d) All of the above

2. Which of the following operating systems is open-source?
    a) Windows
    b) macOS
    c) Linux
    d) Android

3. Which package manager is commonly used in Debian-based Linux distributions like Ubuntu?
    a) APT
    b) DNF
    c) Pacman
    d) YUM

4. What is the purpose of software virtualization?
    a) To run multiple operating systems on a single machine
    b) To install software without an internet connection
    c) To optimize system performance
    d) To increase network security

5. Which Windows feature provides full-disk encryption to protect data?
    a) Windows Firewall
    b) Windows Defender
    c) BitLocker
    d) Windows Update

6. Which macOS feature allows users to make and receive phone calls on a Mac using an iPhone?
    a) Time Machine
    b) iCloud
    c) Handoff
    d) Gatekeeper

7. Which Linux desktop environment is known for its simplicity and elegance?
    a) KDE Plasma

b) XFCE

c) GNOME

d) Cinnamon

8. What is the purpose of a package manager in Linux?

   a) To manage software installations and updates

   b) To provide access to online games

   c) To optimize system performance

   d) To manage hardware drivers

9. Which tool is used to create and manage virtual machines on Windows?

   a) VMware

   b) VirtualBox

   c) Docker

   d) Hyper-V

10. What does the term "CLI" stand for?

    a) Computer Language Interface

    b) Command-Line Interface

    c) Control Logic Input

    d) Centralized Line Instructions

11. Which operating system is developed by Apple Inc. for Macintosh computers?

    a) Windows

    b) Linux

    c) macOS

    d) Android

12. What is the primary purpose of system updates and patches?

    a) To improve hardware performance

    b) To add new features to the operating system

    c) To fix security vulnerabilities and bugs

    d) To update the user interface

13. Which command is commonly used to install software packages on Ubuntu Linux?

    a) apt install

    b) yum install

    c) pacman -S

    d) dnf install

14. Which software management tool is used for configuration management and automation on Linux systems?
    a) Ansible
    b) Puppet
    c) Chef
    d) All of the above

15. What is the purpose of Time Machine on macOS?
    a) To optimize system performance
    b) To backup and restore data
    c) To manage software licenses
    d) To scan for malware

16. What is the function of a package manager in Windows?
    a) To manage device drivers
    b) To install security updates
    c) To manage software installations and updates
    d) To optimize system performance

17. Which Windows feature provides real-time protection against viruses and malware?
    a) Windows Firewall
    b) Windows Update
    c) Windows Defender
    d) BitLocker

18. Which Linux distribution is known for its community-driven and cutting-edge approach?
    a) Ubuntu
    b) Fedora
    c) CentOS
    d) Debian

19. Which macOS feature syncs files, photos, and other data across all Apple devices?
    a) Time Machine
    b) iCloud
    c) Spotlight Search
    d) Continuity

20. Which Linux desktop environment is suitable for older hardware and provides a lightweight user interface?

a) KDE Plasma

b) XFCE

c) Cinnamon

d) GNOME

21. What is the purpose of an operating system's boot loader?

    a) To load the operating system kernel into memory

    b) To manage software installations and updates

    c) To handle system backups

    d) To optimize system performance

22. Which Linux distribution is known for its stability, reliability, and use in server environments?

    a) Ubuntu

    b) Arch Linux

    c) CentOS

    d) Fedora

23. What is the primary function of Windows Update?

    a) To install new software applications

    b) To optimize system performance

    c) To provide new features to the operating system

    d) To deliver security updates and patches

24. Which macOS feature provides automatic and reliable backup to an external storage device?

    a) Time Machine

    b) Handoff

    c) iCloud

    d) Spotlight Search

25. What is the purpose of a software repository in Linux?

    a) To store physical copies of software packages

    b) To manage hardware resources

    c) To provide a centralized location for software installation and updates

    d) To optimize system performance

26. Which Linux distribution is often used for ethical hacking and penetration testing?

    a) Ubuntu

    b) Kali Linux

    c) Fedora

d) Linux Mint

27. Which macOS feature allows users to quickly locate files, applications, and information on the system?

    a) Time Machine

    b) FileVault

    c) Handoff

    d) Spotlight Search

28. Which package manager is commonly used in Arch Linux and its derivatives?

    a) APT

    b) DNF

    c) Pacman

    d) YUM

29. What is the purpose of system restore in Windows?

    a) To backup and restore data files

    b) To revert the system to a previous state (restore point) in case of issues

    c) To create a system backup on an external device

    d) To optimize system performance

30. Which command is used to uninstall software packages on Linux using the APT package manager?

    a) apt uninstall

    b) apt remove

    c) apt delete

    d) apt purge

Security

Computer security is a critical aspect of using and managing computer systems. It involves protecting hardware, software, and data from unauthorized access, misuse, damage, or theft. Understanding computer security principles is essential for maintaining the confidentiality, integrity, and availability of information. Let's delve into the key topics related to computer security:

1. Authentication and Access Control:

Authentication: The process of verifying the identity of a user or entity attempting to access a system or resource. Common authentication methods include passwords, biometrics, smart cards, and multi-factor authentication (MFA).

Access Control: The practice of granting or restricting access to specific resources based on the user's identity, role, or privileges. Access control mechanisms ensure that users only have access to the resources they are authorized to use.

2. Encryption:

Encryption involves converting data into a coded form to prevent unauthorized access. It ensures that even if data is intercepted, it remains unreadable without the decryption key.

End-to-end encryption is commonly used in secure communication applications to protect data while in transit.

3. Firewalls and Intrusion Detection/Prevention Systems (IDS/IPS):

Firewalls are network security devices that control incoming and outgoing network traffic based on predefined security rules.

IDS/IPS monitor network traffic for suspicious or malicious activity and take actions to prevent potential threats.

4. Antivirus and Antimalware Software:

Antivirus and antimalware programs protect against viruses, worms, Trojans, and other malicious software that can infect computers and compromise data.

These programs regularly scan systems and files to detect and remove malware.

5. Patch Management:

Regularly applying software updates and patches is crucial for fixing known security vulnerabilities and improving system security.

Patch management ensures that systems are up to date with the latest security fixes.

6. Secure Web Browsing:

Secure web browsing involves using HTTPS (Hypertext Transfer Protocol Secure) to encrypt data transmitted between the user's browser and the web server.

HTTPS is commonly used for secure online transactions and sensitive information exchange.

7. Social Engineering Awareness:

Social engineering involves manipulating individuals to disclose sensitive information or perform certain actions.

Users must be aware of social engineering tactics like phishing emails and phone calls to avoid falling victim to such attacks.

8. Network Segmentation:

Network segmentation involves dividing a network into smaller, isolated segments to contain potential security breaches and limit the impact of attacks.

It helps prevent lateral movement of attackers within the network.

9. Data Backup and Disaster Recovery:

Regular data backups ensure that critical data can be restored in case of data loss due to hardware failures, malware, or other disasters.

Disaster recovery plans outline procedures for resuming operations after a catastrophic event.

10. User Training and Security Policies:

Educating users about security best practices and potential risks is essential for promoting a security-conscious culture.

Organizations should have well-defined security policies and guidelines to govern data handling, password management, and security procedures.

11. Physical Security:

Physical security measures, such as access control systems, surveillance cameras, and secure entry points, protect physical devices and data storage locations from unauthorized access.

12. Incident Response and Security Monitoring:

Incident response plans outline procedures for detecting, analyzing, and responding to security incidents and breaches.

Security monitoring involves continuous monitoring of network and system activity to detect anomalies and potential threats.

13. Penetration Testing and Vulnerability Assessments:

Penetration testing involves simulating cyber-attacks to identify weaknesses in a system's defenses.

Vulnerability assessments help identify and prioritize potential security vulnerabilities that need to be addressed.

14. Two-Factor Authentication (2FA) and Multi-Factor Authentication (MFA):

Two-Factor Authentication (2FA) and Multi-Factor Authentication (MFA) add an extra layer of security to the authentication process. Users need to provide additional information beyond their passwords, such as a one-time code sent to their mobile device, a fingerprint scan, or a smart card.

2FA and MFA make it harder for attackers to gain unauthorized access, even if they have the user's password.

15. Denial-of-Service (DoS) and Distributed Denial-of-Service (DDoS) Attacks:

Denial-of-Service (DoS) attacks overwhelm a system or network with a high volume of traffic or requests, causing the system to become slow or unavailable.

Distributed Denial-of-Service (DDoS) attacks use multiple compromised devices (botnets) to flood the target with traffic, making it harder to defend against.

16. Ransomware:

Ransomware is a type of malware that encrypts a user's files or locks them out of their system. The attacker demands a ransom to provide the decryption key or unlock the system.

Regular data backups are crucial to mitigate the impact of ransomware attacks.

17. Insider Threats:

Insider threats involve employees or authorized users who intentionally or unintentionally pose security risks to an organization.

Mitigating insider threats involves monitoring user activity, restricting access to sensitive information, and implementing security awareness programs.

18. Secure Email and Phishing Prevention:

Secure email practices involve using encryption for sensitive email communication and being cautious about opening attachments or clicking on links from unknown sources.

Phishing prevention measures include user education about recognizing phishing attempts and implementing email filtering to detect and block phishing emails.

19. Bring Your Own Device (BYOD) Security:

BYOD policies allow employees to use their personal devices for work purposes. Proper security measures must be in place to protect corporate data and ensure device compliance.

Mobile device management and remote wipe capabilities are essential for securing BYOD environments.

20. Zero Trust Security Model:

The Zero Trust security model is based on the principle of "never trust, always verify." It assumes that all users, devices, and network segments are untrusted until proven otherwise.

Zero Trust architectures implement strict access controls and authentication measures to protect against unauthorized access.

21. Security Audits and Compliance:

Regular security audits assess the effectiveness of security controls and identify potential vulnerabilities.

Compliance with industry standards and regulations (e.g., GDPR, HIPAA) ensures that organizations meet specific security requirements.

22. End-User Security Awareness:

Educating end-users about security best practices is crucial for preventing security breaches caused by human error.

Security awareness training covers topics like password hygiene, safe browsing, and social engineering awareness.

23. Security Incident Response Plan:

A security incident response plan outlines the procedures for handling security incidents, including how to detect, respond, and recover from a security breach.

24. Biometric Authentication:

Biometric authentication uses unique physical characteristics, such as fingerprints or facial recognition, to verify a user's identity.

Biometric data cannot be easily replicated, making it a more secure form of authentication.

25. Virtual Private Network (VPN):

A VPN creates an encrypted tunnel between a user's device and a remote server, protecting data transmitted over the internet.

VPNs are commonly used to secure remote connections and protect sensitive information from eavesdropping.

7.1 Physical Security Measures

Physical security measures are designed to protect physical assets, hardware, and data storage locations from unauthorized access, theft, or damage. These measures are essential to complement the cybersecurity efforts in maintaining the overall security of an organization's premises and infrastructure. Let's explore some common physical security measures:

1. Access Control Systems:

Access control systems regulate entry to buildings, rooms, or sensitive areas. This can include using electronic keycards, biometric scanners (fingerprint, iris, or facial recognition), or personal identification numbers (PINs).

2. Surveillance Cameras:

Surveillance cameras are strategically placed to monitor and record activities within and around the premises. They serve as a deterrent to potential intruders and assist in investigating incidents.

3. Security Guards:

Security personnel are stationed at entrances, exits, and critical areas to monitor access, perform patrols, and respond to security incidents.

4. Fencing and Perimeter Security:

Fences and barriers help establish a clear boundary around the facility, making it more difficult for unauthorized individuals to gain access.

5. Security Alarms:

Security alarm systems can be triggered by unauthorized entry, break-ins, or tampering, alerting security personnel or law enforcement agencies.

6. Biometric Locks:

Biometric locks use unique physical characteristics to grant access, enhancing the security of doors, cabinets, or sensitive areas.

7. Mantraps and Access Interlocks:

Mantraps are secure enclosures with two consecutive doors. A person must be verified and authorized to enter the second door, preventing unauthorized access.

8. Environmental Controls:

Environmental controls include measures to protect hardware and data storage from environmental hazards such as fire, water damage, and extreme temperatures.

9. Visitor Management Systems:

Visitor management systems require visitors to register upon entry, providing identification and purpose of visit. This helps track and manage visitors effectively.

10. Secure Storage Cabinets and Safes:

Secure cabinets and safes are used to store valuable assets, sensitive data, and important documents securely.

11. Security Lighting:

Adequate outdoor lighting helps deter unauthorized access and improves visibility during nighttime.

12. Key Management:

Key management practices ensure that access to keys is strictly controlled and monitored.

13. Redundant Power and Data Connections:

Redundancy in power and data connections ensures that critical systems remain operational in case of power outages or network failures.

14. Secure Disposal and Recycling of Hardware:

Proper disposal or recycling of hardware ensures that sensitive data is not accessible after the equipment reaches the end of its lifecycle.

15. Secure Server Rooms and Data Centers:

Server rooms and data centers housing critical infrastructure should have restricted access and environmental controls to protect against unauthorized entry and potential damage.

16. Security Signage:

Signage throughout the premises communicates security policies, access restrictions, and contact information for reporting suspicious activities.

17. Training and Security Awareness:

Employees should be educated about the importance of physical security and their roles in maintaining it.

18. Secure Hardware Asset Management:

Proper hardware asset management ensures that all physical devices and equipment are accounted for, properly labeled, and tracked throughout their lifecycle.

Asset management systems help prevent unauthorized acquisition or disposal of hardware, reducing the risk of data breaches.

19. Secure Trash Disposal and Shredding:

Sensitive documents and media should be properly disposed of using shredders or secure destruction methods to prevent unauthorized access to confidential information.

20. Locking Cabinets and Racks:

Cabinets and racks containing networking equipment, servers, and other critical hardware should be lockable to restrict physical access to authorized personnel only.

21. Reception Area Security:

Security measures should be in place at the reception area to screen and verify visitors before allowing them further access into the facility.

22. Secure Delivery and Loading Zones:

Delivery and loading zones should be monitored and controlled to prevent unauthorized access and ensure the security of incoming and outgoing shipments.

23. Emergency Exit and Panic Bar:

Emergency exits should be clearly marked and equipped with panic bars to allow quick evacuation in case of emergencies while preventing unauthorized entry.

24. Secure Parking Facilities:

Security measures should be implemented in parking areas to prevent theft, vandalism, and unauthorized access to vehicles.

25. Secure Lockers and Personal Storage Areas:

Employees may have personal belongings and devices they need to secure while at work. Providing secure lockers or personal storage areas ensures the safety of their belongings.

26. Bollards and Vehicle Barriers:

Bollards and barriers strategically placed around the premises prevent vehicle-based attacks and protect critical infrastructure from accidental collisions.

27. Biometric Access Control for Data Centers:

Biometric access control at data center entrances adds an extra layer of security to protect against unauthorized access to sensitive data and equipment.

28. Security Awareness Training for Employees:

Regular security awareness training educates employees about the importance of physical security, identifies potential risks, and promotes a security-conscious culture.

29. Secure Remote Working Policies:

For employees working remotely, organizations should establish secure remote working policies and provide guidelines for securing equipment and data outside the office environment.

30. Regular Security Audits and Testing:

Conducting regular security audits and testing of physical security measures helps identify vulnerabilities and weaknesses that need to be addressed.

31. Incident Response and Emergency Procedures:

Well-defined incident response and emergency procedures outline the actions to be taken in case of security breaches, natural disasters, or other emergencies.

32. Compliance with Regulatory Standards:

Ensuring compliance with industry-specific regulations and standards related to physical security helps meet legal requirements and industry best practices.

7.2 Network Security Fundamentals

Network security is essential for safeguarding data and resources from unauthorized access, attacks, and potential breaches. It involves implementing various measures to protect networks, devices, and data during transmission and storage. Here are some fundamental concepts of network security:

1. Firewall:

Firewalls are network security devices that control and monitor incoming and outgoing network traffic based on predefined security rules. They act as a barrier between a trusted internal network and untrusted external networks, such as the internet.

2. Virtual Private Network (VPN):

VPNs create encrypted tunnels between a user's device and a remote server, ensuring secure communication over untrusted networks. VPNs are commonly used for remote work, allowing employees to access the organization's network securely.

3. Intrusion Detection System (IDS) and Intrusion Prevention System (IPS):

IDS and IPS monitor network traffic for suspicious or malicious activity. IDS detects potential security breaches, while IPS takes active measures to prevent unauthorized access or attacks.

4. Network Segmentation:

Network segmentation involves dividing a network into smaller, isolated segments. This helps contain potential security breaches and limits the impact of attacks.

5. Secure Sockets Layer/Transport Layer Security (SSL/TLS):

SSL/TLS protocols provide secure encryption for data transmitted over the internet. They are commonly used for securing online transactions and sensitive information exchange.

6. Access Control Lists (ACLs):

ACLs are rules that control network traffic flow, allowing or denying access based on various criteria such as IP addresses, ports, or protocols.

7. Network Address Translation (NAT):

NAT translates private IP addresses of devices within a local network to a single public IP address used for communication with external networks, enhancing network security by hiding internal addresses.

8. Secure Remote Access:

Secure remote access solutions, such as secure VPNs and multi-factor authentication (MFA), allow remote users to access the network and resources securely.

9. Wireless Network Security:

Wireless networks should be protected with strong authentication and encryption, such as WPA2 or WPA3, to prevent unauthorized access.

10. Network Monitoring and Logging:

Network monitoring tools continuously track network activity to detect anomalies and potential security threats. Logging records events and activities for analysis and auditing purposes.

11. Denial-of-Service (DoS) and Distributed Denial-of-Service (DDoS) Mitigation:

DoS and DDoS attacks overwhelm networks with high volumes of traffic. Mitigation measures, such as rate limiting and traffic filtering, help protect against such attacks.

12. Network Security Policies:

Organizations should establish clear network security policies that outline acceptable use, access controls, and procedures for handling security incidents.

13. Patch Management:

Regularly applying security patches to network devices, routers, switches, and servers helps fix known vulnerabilities and strengthen network security.

14. Network Security Audits and Penetration Testing:

Network security audits and penetration testing identify weaknesses and vulnerabilities in the network infrastructure, allowing organizations to address potential risks proactively.

15. Data Encryption in Transit and at Rest:

Encrypting data during transmission and storage ensures that even if intercepted, the data remains unreadable without the decryption key.

16. Network Access Control (NAC):

Network Access Control (NAC) solutions enforce policies that determine which devices and users are allowed to access the network. NAC ensures that only authorized and compliant devices can connect to the network.

17. Port Security:

Port security is a feature on network switches that restricts the number of MAC addresses allowed on a specific switch port. This prevents unauthorized devices from connecting to the network through that port.

18. Network Hardening:

Network hardening involves configuring network devices and systems to minimize potential vulnerabilities and reduce the attack surface. This includes disabling unnecessary services, changing default settings, and implementing strong authentication methods.

19. Network Authentication Protocols:

Network authentication protocols, such as RADIUS (Remote Authentication Dial-In User Service) and TACACS+ (Terminal Access Controller Access Control System Plus), provide secure authentication for network access.

20. Network Security Monitoring and Incident Response:

Network security monitoring involves continuous monitoring of network traffic, logs, and events to detect and respond to security incidents promptly. Incident response plans outline the actions to be taken in case of a security breach.

21. Network Security Appliances:

Network security appliances, such as Unified Threat Management (UTM) devices and Next-Generation Firewalls (NGFW), integrate multiple security functions (e.g., firewall, antivirus, intrusion prevention) into a single device for efficient protection.

22. Secure DNS Resolution:

Secure Domain Name System (DNS) resolution ensures that DNS queries and responses are protected from tampering or interception, reducing the risk of DNS-related attacks.

23. Network Behavior Analysis (NBA):

Network Behavior Analysis (NBA) solutions monitor network traffic to identify abnormal behavior and potential threats that may not be detected by traditional signature-based security measures.

24. Security Information and Event Management (SIEM):

SIEM solutions aggregate and analyze log data from various network devices and systems to provide a comprehensive view of network security and potential security incidents.

25. Network Forensics:

Network forensics involves the collection and analysis of network data to investigate security incidents, identify the source of an attack, and understand the extent of the breach.

26. Redundancy and High Availability:

Redundancy and high availability ensure that critical network components have backup systems in place to maintain network functionality in case of hardware failures or network disruptions.

27. VLAN (Virtual Local Area Network) Segmentation:

VLAN segmentation separates different network traffic into virtual networks, enhancing security by isolating sensitive data from other parts of the network.

28. Network Security Awareness Training:

Network security awareness training educates employees about common security threats, such as phishing and social engineering, to prevent security breaches caused by human error.

29. Mobile Device Security:

Mobile device security measures, such as mobile device management (MDM) and containerization, protect data and applications on mobile devices used to access the network.

30. Network Policy Enforcement:

Network policy enforcement ensures that network traffic adheres to established security policies and access controls, reducing the risk of unauthorized access and data leakage.

7.3 Computer Security Threats and Countermeasures

Computer systems face a myriad of security threats that can compromise the confidentiality, integrity, and availability of data. Understanding these threats and implementing appropriate countermeasures is crucial for maintaining a secure computing environment. Here are some common computer security threats and the corresponding countermeasures:

1. Malware:

Threat: Malware includes viruses, worms, Trojans, ransomware, and other malicious software designed to disrupt, damage, or steal data.

Countermeasure: Install and regularly update antivirus and antimalware software. Regularly apply security patches to close known vulnerabilities. Educate users about safe browsing practices and avoiding suspicious email attachments or downloads.

2. Phishing Attacks:

Threat: Phishing is a social engineering attack where attackers impersonate legitimate entities to trick users into revealing sensitive information, such as login credentials or financial data.

Countermeasure: Train users to recognize phishing emails and websites. Implement email filtering to detect and block phishing attempts. Use two-factor authentication (2FA) to add an extra layer of security to login processes.

3. Insider Threats:

Threat: Insider threats involve trusted individuals with authorized access to systems who misuse their privileges or inadvertently cause security breaches.

Countermeasure: Implement the principle of least privilege to restrict access to only what is necessary. Monitor user activity and detect unusual behavior. Conduct security awareness training to educate employees about potential security risks.

4. Denial-of-Service (DoS) and Distributed Denial-of-Service (DDoS) Attacks:

Threat: DoS and DDoS attacks overwhelm systems with excessive traffic, causing services to become unavailable.

Countermeasure: Deploy firewalls and intrusion prevention systems to detect and block suspicious traffic. Use load balancers and traffic filtering to mitigate the impact of DDoS attacks.

5. Data Breaches:

Threat: Data breaches occur when sensitive information is accessed, disclosed, or stolen without authorization.

Countermeasure: Encrypt sensitive data both in transit and at rest. Implement access controls and regular security audits to identify vulnerabilities. Develop and practice incident response plans to respond quickly to data breaches.

6. Social Engineering Attacks:

Threat: Social engineering involves manipulating individuals to divulge sensitive information or perform actions that compromise security.

Countermeasure: Provide security awareness training to employees to recognize and avoid social engineering tactics. Encourage a culture of skepticism and verify the identity of requestors before disclosing sensitive information.

7. Unauthorized Access:

Threat: Unauthorized access occurs when individuals gain entry to systems, applications, or data without proper authorization.

Countermeasure: Enforce strong password policies and implement multi-factor authentication (MFA). Use network segmentation and access controls to limit unauthorized access.

8. Man-in-the-Middle (MITM) Attacks:

Threat: MITM attacks intercept and alter communication between two parties without their knowledge.

Countermeasure: Use encryption protocols like SSL/TLS to secure communication channels. Verify digital certificates to ensure the authenticity of websites and servers.

9. Zero-Day Exploits:

Threat: Zero-day exploits target unknown vulnerabilities that have not been patched by software vendors.

Countermeasure: Apply regular software updates and patches promptly. Use intrusion detection systems to detect potential zero-day attacks.

10. Physical Theft and Tampering:

Threat: Physical theft or tampering can lead to unauthorized access or data breaches.

Countermeasure: Implement physical security measures, such as access controls, surveillance cameras, and secure storage, to protect against theft and tampering.

11. Insider Data Leakage:

Threat: Insider data leakage occurs when authorized users intentionally or unintentionally share sensitive information with unauthorized individuals or entities.

Countermeasure: Implement data loss prevention (DLP) solutions to monitor and control the movement of sensitive data. Restrict access to sensitive information on a need-to-know basis. Conduct periodic user access reviews.

12. Credential Theft:

Threat: Credential theft involves stealing login credentials to gain unauthorized access to accounts or systems.

Countermeasure: Encourage strong password practices, including the use of complex passwords and password managers. Implement multi-factor authentication (MFA) to add an extra layer of security to account logins.

13. Eavesdropping and Network Sniffing:

Threat: Eavesdropping and network sniffing involve intercepting and capturing network traffic to gather sensitive information.

Countermeasure: Use encryption protocols like SSL/TLS to secure data transmitted over networks. Segment networks and use VPNs for secure communication over untrusted networks.

14. Software Vulnerabilities:

Threat: Software vulnerabilities are weaknesses in software code that can be exploited by attackers to gain unauthorized access or control over systems.

Countermeasure: Regularly apply security patches and updates to fix known vulnerabilities. Conduct vulnerability assessments and penetration testing to identify and address software weaknesses.

15. Web Application Attacks:

Threat: Web application attacks, such as SQL injection and cross-site scripting (XSS), target vulnerabilities in web applications to gain unauthorized access or manipulate data.

Countermeasure: Secure web applications through secure coding practices and regular security testing. Implement web application firewalls (WAFs) to detect and block malicious web traffic.

16. Ransomware Attacks:

Threat: Ransomware encrypts data and demands a ransom for decryption, preventing users from accessing their files.

Countermeasure: Regularly back up critical data and store backups securely offline. Train users to be cautious of suspicious email attachments and links.

17. Internet of Things (IoT) Vulnerabilities:

Threat: IoT devices often have weak security controls and can become entry points for attackers to gain access to networks.

Countermeasure: Secure IoT devices with strong passwords and firmware updates. Segment IoT devices from critical systems to limit potential damage.

18. Cloud Security Risks:

Threat: Cloud services may expose data to unauthorized access if not properly configured or secured.

Countermeasure: Implement strong access controls and encryption for cloud data. Regularly review and monitor cloud service configurations for security compliance.

19. Advanced Persistent Threats (APTs):

Threat: APTs are stealthy and long-term targeted attacks aimed at gaining persistent access to systems.

Countermeasure: Use advanced threat detection solutions, conduct threat hunting, and implement network segmentation to contain APTs.

20. Supply Chain Attacks:

Threat: Supply chain attacks exploit vulnerabilities in software and hardware supply chains to distribute malicious components.

Countermeasure: Vet suppliers and perform security assessments on software and hardware components to reduce the risk of supply chain attacks.

21. Social Media Risks:

Threat: Social media platforms may be used for social engineering attacks and to gather information for targeted attacks.

Countermeasure: Educate users about sharing sensitive information on social media and the potential risks associated with social engineering.

Quiz

1. What is the primary purpose of antivirus software?
   a) Protecting hardware from physical damage
   b) Preventing unauthorized access to networks
   c) Detecting and removing malicious software
   d) Encrypting data during transmission

2. Phishing is a type of attack that involves:
   a) Manipulating individuals to disclose sensitive information
   b) Overloading a system with excessive traffic
   c) Intercepting network traffic to steal data
   d) Gaining unauthorized access to a network

3. Which security measure creates an encrypted tunnel for secure communication over untrusted networks?
   a) VPN
   b) Firewall
   c) Intrusion Detection System (IDS)
   d) Access Control List (ACL)

4. What is the purpose of a firewall in a network security context?
   a) Encrypting data during transmission
   b) Monitoring and controlling network traffic based on security rules
   c) Preventing unauthorized physical access to devices
   d) Identifying and blocking phishing emails

5. Malware that encrypts a user's files and demands a ransom for decryption is known as:
   a) Phishing
   b) Trojan
   c) Virus
   d) Ransomware

6. Which type of attack aims to overwhelm a system with a high volume of traffic to make it unavailable?
   a) Phishing attack
   b) Denial-of-Service (DoS) attack
   c) Man-in-the-Middle (MITM) attack
   d) SQL injection attack

7. What is the recommended practice for creating strong passwords?

    a) Using common dictionary words

    b) Using the same password for multiple accounts

    c) Including a mix of uppercase and lowercase letters, numbers, and special characters

    d) Keeping passwords written on sticky notes near the computer

8. What is the purpose of Multi-Factor Authentication (MFA)?

    a) Encrypting data during transmission

    b) Protecting against physical theft of devices

    c) Adding an extra layer of security by requiring multiple forms of authentication

    d) Preventing unauthorized access to networks

9. Insider threats involve:

    a) Gaining unauthorized access to networks from remote locations

    b) Manipulating individuals to disclose sensitive information

    c) Unauthorized access to networks through physical intrusion

    d) Trusted individuals with authorized access causing security breaches

10. What is the primary purpose of a Network Access Control (NAC) system?

    a) Protecting against physical theft of devices

    b) Encrypting data during transmission

    c) Controlling and monitoring devices' access to the network based on security policies

    d) Preventing unauthorized access to networks

11. Social engineering attacks involve:

    a) Overloading a system with excessive traffic

    b) Manipulating individuals to reveal sensitive information or perform actions

    c) Intercepting network traffic to steal data

    d) Gaining unauthorized access to a network

12. What is the term for the practice of dividing a network into smaller isolated segments?

    a) Network segmentation

    b) VPN tunneling

    c) Firewall filtering

    d) Intrusion Detection

13. What is the purpose of data encryption in network security?

    a) Protecting against physical theft of devices

    b) Controlling and monitoring devices' access to the network

c) Securing data during transmission to prevent eavesdropping

d) Identifying and blocking phishing emails

14. What type of attack involves manipulating individuals to disclose sensitive information through deceptive means?

    a) Phishing attack

    b) Denial-of-Service (DoS) attack

    c) Malware attack

    d) SQL injection attack

15. Which security measure involves creating strong boundaries around a network to limit unauthorized access?

    a) VPN

    b) Firewall

    c) Intrusion Detection System (IDS)

    d) Access Control List (ACL)

16. What is the purpose of intrusion detection systems (IDS)?

    a) Encrypting data during transmission

    b) Monitoring and alerting about suspicious or malicious activity on the network

    c) Controlling access to network resources

    d) Detecting and removing malicious software

17. Which type of malware disguises itself as a legitimate software but carries out malicious activities in the background?

    a) Virus

    b) Worm

    c) Trojan

    d) Ransomware

18. What does SSL/TLS stand for in the context of network security?

    a) Secure Sockets Layer/Transport Layer Security

    b) Secure Security Layer/Transport Layer System

    c) Secure System Layer/Transport Layer Security

    d) Secure Secure Layer/Transmission Level System

19. What is the purpose of using encryption for data at rest?

    a) Protecting against physical theft of devices

    b) Controlling and monitoring devices' access to the network

c) Securing data during transmission to prevent eavesdropping

d) Safeguarding data stored on storage devices from unauthorized access

20. Which type of attack involves intercepting and capturing network traffic to gather sensitive information?

    a) Phishing attack

    b) Denial-of-Service (DoS) attack

    c) Man-in-the-Middle (MITM) attack

    d) SQL injection attack

21. What is the best practice for handling suspicious email attachments?

    a) Open the attachment to check its content.

    b) Delete the email without opening the attachment.

    c) Forward the email to colleagues for further inspection.

    d) Upload the attachment to an online virus scanner for analysis.

22. What type of security measure involves limiting access to network resources based on user roles and permissions?

    a) Multi-Factor Authentication (MFA)

    b) Access Control List (ACL)

    c) Intrusion Detection System (IDS)

    d) Phishing attack

23. What is the purpose of conducting regular security audits and vulnerability assessments?

    a) Encrypting data during transmission

    b) Monitoring and controlling network traffic based on security rules

    c) Identifying weaknesses and potential security risks in the network

    d) Detecting and removing malicious software

24. What is the term for a persistent and targeted cyber-attack aimed at gaining unauthorized access to systems?

    a) Phishing attack

    b) Advanced Persistent Threat (APT)

    c) Man-in-the-Middle (MITM) attack

    d) Denial-of-Service (DoS) attack

25. Which security measure involves verifying the identity of individuals or devices before granting access to resources?

    a) Intrusion Detection System (IDS)

b) Multi-Factor Authentication (MFA)

c) Phishing attack

d) Firewall

26. What is the primary purpose of data loss prevention (DLP) solutions?

    a) Preventing unauthorized access to networks

    b) Detecting and blocking phishing emails

    c) Controlling and monitoring data movement to prevent data leakage

    d) Monitoring network traffic for suspicious activity

27. Which type of attack targets web applications by injecting malicious code to exploit vulnerabilities?

    a) Phishing attack

    b) Denial-of-Service (DoS) attack

    c) Man-in-the-Middle (MITM) attack

    d) SQL injection attack

28. What is the term for the practice of limiting user access to only the resources necessary for their job role?

    a) Principle of least privilege

    b) Multi-Factor Authentication (MFA)

    c) Social engineering

    d) Network segmentation

29. What security measure involves creating secure boundaries around data to protect it from unauthorized access?

    a) VPN

    b) Firewall

    c) Encryption

    d) Antivirus

30. What is the primary purpose of conducting security awareness training for employees?

    a) Preventing physical theft of devices

    b) Educating employees about cybersecurity best practices

    c) Detecting and removing malware from devices

    d) Encrypting data during transmission

Software Troubleshooting

Software troubleshooting involves identifying and resolving issues related to software applications, operating systems, and other software components. Here are some common software troubleshooting topics:

1. Application Crashes:

Issue: Applications may crash or become unresponsive due to software bugs, conflicting processes, or insufficient system resources.

Troubleshooting: Check for software updates or patches. Close unnecessary background processes. Verify system requirements and available resources.

2. Blue Screen of Death (BSOD):

Issue: BSOD indicates a critical system error on Windows systems, often caused by faulty hardware drivers or hardware issues.

Troubleshooting: Update or reinstall hardware drivers. Check for hardware problems using diagnostic tools.

3. Slow System Performance:

Issue: Slow system performance may result from background processes, insufficient RAM, malware, or fragmented storage.

Troubleshooting: Close unnecessary programs and background processes. Scan for malware. Upgrade RAM or replace the storage device if needed.

4. Software Compatibility Issues:

Issue: Some software may not function correctly or crash when running on specific operating systems or hardware configurations.

Troubleshooting: Check software compatibility with the operating system and hardware. Use compatibility modes if available.

5. Internet Connection Problems:

Issue: Internet connectivity issues may arise due to network settings, router problems, or ISP-related issues.

Troubleshooting: Restart the router. Verify network settings. Contact the ISP for connectivity problems.

6. Unresponsive Applications:

Issue: Applications may become unresponsive due to high CPU usage, memory leaks, or resource conflicts.

Troubleshooting: Close the unresponsive application. Monitor system resources using Task Manager.

7. Error Messages:

Issue: Error messages may indicate software issues, missing files, or incorrect configurations.

Troubleshooting: Investigate error messages for clues. Search online for specific error codes or messages.

8. Application Installation Problems:

Issue: Some applications may fail to install correctly due to missing dependencies or system requirements.

Troubleshooting: Check system requirements. Install any required dependencies. Disable antivirus during installation.

9. Application Configuration Errors:

Issue: Misconfigured application settings may cause unexpected behavior or errors.

Troubleshooting: Review application settings and preferences. Reset to default if necessary.

10. File and Folder Permissions:

Issue: Inadequate file and folder permissions can lead to access problems or security vulnerabilities.

Troubleshooting: Adjust file and folder permissions as needed to ensure proper access rights.

11. Missing or Corrupted System Files:

Issue: Missing or corrupted system files can lead to application errors or system instability.

Troubleshooting: Use system file checking tools like "sfc /scannow" on Windows or "fsck" on Linux to check and repair system files.

12. Password Recovery:

Issue: Forgetting passwords can lock users out of their accounts or encrypted files.

Troubleshooting: Use password recovery options provided by the application or contact the system administrator for assistance.

13. Disk Space Issues:

Issue: Low disk space can cause applications to malfunction or prevent the installation of new software.

Troubleshooting: Free up disk space by removing unnecessary files or expanding storage capacity.

14. Printer Problems:

Issue: Printers may fail to print or produce poor-quality output due to driver issues or incorrect configurations.

Troubleshooting: Check printer connections and settings. Reinstall or update printer drivers if necessary.

15. Malware Infections:

Issue: Malware infections can cause system instability, data loss, or unauthorized access.

Troubleshooting: Use reputable antivirus and antimalware tools to scan and remove malware.

16. Application-specific Errors:

Issue: Some applications may display specific errors related to their functions.

Troubleshooting: Refer to application documentation or online resources for troubleshooting guidance.

17. System Restore and Backup:

Issue: Data loss or system corruption can be mitigated using system restore points or regular backups.

Troubleshooting: Create system restore points before making major changes. Implement regular data backups.

18. Boot Problems:

Issue: Boot problems may prevent the system from starting properly.

Troubleshooting: Check the boot order in the BIOS/UEFI settings. Use boot repair tools or recovery options.

19. Software Updates and Patches:

Issue: Failure to apply software updates and patches can lead to security vulnerabilities and software issues.

Troubleshooting: Regularly install updates and patches for the operating system and applications.

20. Application Freezing:

Issue: Applications may freeze or become unresponsive due to various reasons, such as resource exhaustion or software bugs.

Troubleshooting: Close the unresponsive application using Task Manager. Investigate resource usage and consider updating or reinstalling the application.

8.1 Troubleshooting Microsoft Windows

Microsoft Windows is one of the most widely used operating systems, and users may encounter various issues while using it. Here are some common troubleshooting topics for Microsoft Windows:

1. Blue Screen of Death (BSOD):

Issue: BSOD indicates a critical system error and may display error codes like "DRIVER_IRQL_NOT_LESS_OR_EQUAL" or "PAGE_FAULT_IN_NONPAGED_AREA."

Troubleshooting: Identify recently installed hardware or drivers causing conflicts. Update or reinstall faulty drivers. Check for hardware issues.

2. Slow Startup and Shutdown:

Issue: Windows may take a long time to boot or shut down.

Troubleshooting: Disable unnecessary startup programs. Check for disk errors using "chkdsk" utility. Update drivers.

3. Application Compatibility Issues:

Issue: Some applications may not work correctly on certain versions of Windows.

Troubleshooting: Use compatibility mode or check for updates from the application developer.

4. Network Connection Problems:

Issue: Network connectivity issues can prevent internet access or local network connections.

Troubleshooting: Verify network adapter settings. Restart the router. Reset TCP/IP using "netsh" command.

5. Windows Update Failures:

Issue: Windows updates may fail to install or encounter errors.

Troubleshooting: Run Windows Update Troubleshooter. Manually reset Windows Update components. Check for sufficient disk space.

6. Missing or Corrupted System Files:

Issue: Missing or corrupted system files can cause various errors.

Troubleshooting: Run "sfc /scannow" to repair system files. Use DISM tool for more extensive repairs.

7. Driver Issues:

Issue: Outdated or faulty drivers can lead to hardware malfunctions.

Troubleshooting: Update drivers using Device Manager or download from manufacturer's website.

8. Windows Activation Problems:

Issue: Windows may display activation errors when the license is not valid or activation servers are unreachable.

Troubleshooting: Check internet connectivity for online activation. Use the "slmgr.vbs" command for manual activation.

9. Windows Store App Problems:

Issue: Windows Store apps may not install or function correctly.

Troubleshooting: Reset Windows Store cache. Re-register Windows Store apps using PowerShell.

10. System Restore Failure:

Issue: System Restore may fail to complete or encounter errors.

Troubleshooting: Check available disk space. Disable antivirus during System Restore. Run System Restore in Safe Mode.

11. File and Folder Permission Issues:

Issue: Inadequate file and folder permissions can restrict access or cause errors.

Troubleshooting: Adjust file and folder permissions using "Security" tab in file properties.

12. Windows Explorer Crashes:

Issue: Windows Explorer may crash or become unresponsive.

Troubleshooting: Restart Windows Explorer from Task Manager. Disable problematic shell extensions.

13. Windows Recovery Options:

Issue: Windows Recovery Options allow users to troubleshoot startup issues, system restore, and repair installations.

Troubleshooting: Use Windows Recovery Environment (WinRE) to access various recovery tools.

14. Windows Disk Cleanup and Defragmentation:

Issue: Over time, temporary files and fragmented data can slow down the system.

Troubleshooting: Use Disk Cleanup to remove temporary and unnecessary files. Run Disk Defragmenter to optimize the storage drive.

15. Windows Safe Mode:

Issue: Windows Safe Mode allows users to troubleshoot issues by starting the system with minimal drivers and services.

Troubleshooting: Boot into Safe Mode to diagnose and fix problems caused by third-party software or drivers.

16. Windows System File Checker (sfc):

Issue: The System File Checker (sfc) tool checks and repairs corrupted or missing system files.

Troubleshooting: Run "sfc /scannow" in an elevated Command Prompt to scan and fix system file issues.

17. Windows Event Viewer:

Issue: The Windows Event Viewer logs system events, errors, and warnings that can help diagnose problems.

Troubleshooting: Analyze Event Viewer logs for relevant error messages and event details.

18. Windows Device Manager:

Issue: Device Manager allows users to manage hardware devices and drivers.

Troubleshooting: Use Device Manager to update, roll back, or uninstall faulty drivers.

19. Windows Task Manager:

Issue: Task Manager provides real-time monitoring of system performance and active processes.

Troubleshooting: Identify resource-hungry processes using Task Manager and terminate them if necessary.

20. Windows Memory Diagnostic:

Issue: Memory-related issues can cause system crashes and instability.

Troubleshooting: Run Windows Memory Diagnostic to check for memory problems.

21. Windows System Restore:

Issue: Windows System Restore allows users to revert the system to a previous state when it was working correctly.

Troubleshooting: Use System Restore to undo recent changes that might be causing issues.

22. Windows Power Options:

Issue: Power-related settings can impact system performance and battery life.

Troubleshooting: Adjust Power Options to optimize system performance or battery life.

23. Windows User Account Control (UAC):

Issue: User Account Control helps prevent unauthorized changes to the system but can sometimes interfere with installations.

Troubleshooting: Temporarily disable UAC to perform specific tasks that require elevated privileges.

24. Windows Reset and Refresh:

Issue: Windows Reset and Refresh options allow users to reinstall the operating system or restore it to a factory-fresh state.

Troubleshooting: Use Windows Reset or Refresh as a last resort when other troubleshooting methods fail.

25. Windows Command Prompt and PowerShell:

Issue: Command Prompt and PowerShell provide powerful command-line tools for troubleshooting and system management.

Troubleshooting: Use Command Prompt and PowerShell to execute advanced commands and scripts for specific troubleshooting tasks.

8.2 Troubleshooting Other Operating Systems

In addition to Microsoft Windows, there are other popular operating systems, such as macOS and various Linux distributions. Troubleshooting these operating systems involves understanding their unique features and tools. Here are some common troubleshooting topics for other operating systems:

1. macOS Boot Issues:

Issue: macOS may encounter boot problems, such as a flashing folder icon or a prohibitory sign.

Troubleshooting: Boot into macOS Recovery mode. Use Disk Utility to repair disk or file system errors. Reinstall macOS if needed.

2. Linux Kernel Panics:

Issue: Linux kernel panics occur when the operating system encounters a critical error and cannot recover.

Troubleshooting: Analyze kernel panic logs. Check hardware compatibility and kernel modules.

3. Application Compatibility on macOS and Linux:

Issue: Some applications may not be compatible with macOS or certain Linux distributions.

Troubleshooting: Check for alternative applications compatible with the operating system. Use virtualization or emulation for running Windows-specific applications.

4. Linux Package Management Issues:

Issue: Problems with package management systems, such as APT or DNF, can occur during software installation or updates.

Troubleshooting: Update package lists and repositories. Resolve dependency issues. Verify internet connectivity.

5. macOS or Linux Freezing and Unresponsiveness:

Issue: The system may freeze or become unresponsive due to various factors.

Troubleshooting: Identify resource-intensive processes using Activity Monitor (macOS) or System Monitor (Linux). Close unresponsive applications.

6. macOS or Linux Wi-Fi and Network Problems:

Issue: Wi-Fi connectivity issues can occur on macOS or Linux systems.

Troubleshooting: Check network settings and Wi-Fi connections. Restart network services. Update network drivers.

7. Linux File System Errors:

Issue: Linux file system errors may result from improper shutdown or disk issues.

Troubleshooting: Use "fsck" utility to repair file system errors. Check disk health using SMART tools.

8. Linux Display and Graphics Problems:

Issue: Graphics driver issues can cause display problems, such as screen flickering or low resolution.

Troubleshooting: Update or reinstall graphics drivers. Configure display settings.

9. macOS Time Machine Backup and Restore:

Issue: Time Machine backups may fail, or restoration may encounter errors.

Troubleshooting: Verify backup disk health. Restart Time Machine services. Use Time Machine Recovery to restore.

10. Linux User Account and Permissions:

Issue: Linux users may encounter permissions issues when accessing files or executing programs.

Troubleshooting: Adjust file and directory permissions. Check user groups and permissions.

11. macOS Time Machine Backup and Restore:

Issue: Time Machine backups may fail, or restoration may encounter errors.

Troubleshooting: Verify backup disk health. Restart Time Machine services. Use Time Machine Recovery to restore.

12. Linux Bootloader Issues:

Issue: Bootloader problems can prevent the system from starting.

149

Troubleshooting: Repair or reinstall the bootloader using tools like GRUB (Grand Unified Bootloader).

13. macOS and Linux Terminal Commands:

Issue: Terminal commands and scripts can encounter syntax errors or incorrect usage.

Troubleshooting: Verify command syntax. Use "man" command for manual pages and help.

14. macOS or Linux Hardware Compatibility:

Issue: Hardware components may not be fully compatible with macOS or specific Linux distributions.

Troubleshooting: Check hardware compatibility lists. Update kernel and drivers for better hardware support.

15. macOS Spotlight and Linux Desktop Search:

Issue: Search functions may not work correctly or index files as expected.

Troubleshooting: Rebuild search index. Verify file indexing settings.

16. macOS Time Machine Backup and Restore:

Issue: Time Machine backups may fail, or restoration may encounter errors.

Troubleshooting: Verify backup disk health. Restart Time Machine services. Use Time Machine Recovery to restore.

17. Linux Bootloader Issues:

Issue: Bootloader problems can prevent the system from starting.

Troubleshooting: Repair or reinstall the bootloader using tools like GRUB (Grand Unified Bootloader).

18. macOS and Linux Terminal Commands:

Issue: Terminal commands and scripts can encounter syntax errors or incorrect usage.

Troubleshooting: Verify command syntax. Use "man" command for manual pages and help.

19. macOS or Linux Hardware Compatibility:

Issue: Hardware components may not be fully compatible with macOS or specific Linux distributions.

Troubleshooting: Check hardware compatibility lists. Update kernel and drivers for better hardware support.

20. macOS Spotlight and Linux Desktop Search:

Issue: Search functions may not work correctly or index files as expected.

Troubleshooting: Rebuild search index. Verify file indexing settings.

21. Linux Audio and Sound Issues:

Issue: Sound may not work correctly on Linux systems due to driver or configuration problems.

Troubleshooting: Check audio settings. Install or update audio drivers. Verify sound card compatibility.

22. macOS Time Zone and Date/Time Settings:

Issue: Incorrect time zone or date/time settings can cause synchronization problems.

Troubleshooting: Adjust time zone and date/time settings manually or use network time synchronization.

23. Linux Graphic User Interface (GUI) Problems:

Issue: Linux GUI may freeze or behave erratically due to graphics driver issues.

Troubleshooting: Update graphics drivers. Test different window managers or desktop environments.

24. macOS or Linux Battery Drainage:

Issue: Laptops may experience excessive battery drain.

Troubleshooting: Identify power-hungry processes using Activity Monitor (macOS) or System Monitor (Linux). Adjust power settings.

25. Linux Kernel Module Errors:

Issue: Linux kernel modules may fail to load or cause system instability.

Troubleshooting: Check kernel module dependencies. Update or reinstall kernel modules.

26. macOS Time Machine Backup and Restore:

Issue: Time Machine backups may fail, or restoration may encounter errors.

Troubleshooting: Verify backup disk health. Restart Time Machine services. Use Time Machine Recovery to restore.

27. Linux Bootloader Issues:

Issue: Bootloader problems can prevent the system from starting.

Troubleshooting: Repair or reinstall the bootloader using tools like GRUB (Grand Unified Bootloader).

28. macOS and Linux Terminal Commands:

Issue: Terminal commands and scripts can encounter syntax errors or incorrect usage.

Troubleshooting: Verify command syntax. Use "man" command for manual pages and help.

29. macOS or Linux Hardware Compatibility:

Issue: Hardware components may not be fully compatible with macOS or specific Linux distributions.

Troubleshooting: Check hardware compatibility lists. Update kernel and drivers for better hardware support.

30. macOS Spotlight and Linux Desktop Search:

Issue: Search functions may not work correctly or index files as expected.

Troubleshooting: Rebuild search index. Verify file indexing settings.

8.3 Troubleshooting Mobile OS

Mobile operating systems, such as Android and iOS, power smartphones and tablets. Troubleshooting mobile OS issues can improve device performance and resolve software-related problems. Here are some common troubleshooting topics for mobile operating systems:

1. Device Battery Drainage:

Issue: Battery life may be shorter than expected due to various factors, including background processes and app usage.

Troubleshooting: Identify power-hungry apps using battery settings. Close unused apps and disable unnecessary background processes.

2. App Crashes and Freezes:

Issue: Apps may crash or become unresponsive, leading to an interrupted user experience.

Troubleshooting: Clear app cache and data. Update the app to the latest version. Reinstall the app if the issue persists.

3. Slow Performance:

Issue: The device may become sluggish or slow, affecting overall performance.

Troubleshooting: Free up storage space by deleting unnecessary files and apps. Restart the device regularly. Consider a factory reset as a last resort.

4. Network Connectivity Problems:

Issue: Mobile devices may experience Wi-Fi or mobile data connectivity issues.

Troubleshooting: Toggle Wi-Fi and mobile data settings. Restart the device or reset network settings if needed.

5. Mobile OS Updates and Patches:

Issue: Failure to install OS updates may lead to security vulnerabilities and performance issues.

Troubleshooting: Check for available updates in the device settings. Download and install the latest updates.

6. Storage Space Running Out:

Issue: Insufficient storage space can prevent app installations and system updates.

Troubleshooting: Delete unused apps, media, and files. Use cloud storage or external storage options.

7. Unresponsive Touchscreen:

Issue: The touchscreen may become unresponsive or register incorrect taps.

Troubleshooting: Clean the screen surface. Restart the device. Update the device firmware if available.

8. Mobile OS Performance Optimization:

Issue: Mobile OS may slow down over time due to accumulated temporary files and system data.

Troubleshooting: Use built-in performance optimization tools or third-party apps to clean up and optimize the device.

9. Mobile App Permissions and Privacy:

Issue: Apps may request excessive permissions or access user data without consent.

Troubleshooting: Review app permissions in the device settings. Avoid installing apps from unknown sources.

10. Mobile OS Data Backup and Restore:

Issue: Data loss may occur due to accidental deletion or device issues.

Troubleshooting: Enable automatic data backup to cloud services or use built-in backup options. Restore data from backups if necessary.

11. Mobile App Compatibility:

Issue: Some apps may not be compatible with specific mobile OS versions or device models.

Troubleshooting: Check app compatibility in the app store. Contact the app developer for support.

12. Mobile OS Security and Antivirus:

Issue: Mobile devices are susceptible to malware and security threats.

Troubleshooting: Install reputable antivirus apps. Avoid downloading apps from unofficial sources.

13. Mobile App Updates and Troubleshooting:

Issue: Some apps may malfunction or encounter bugs due to outdated versions.

Troubleshooting: Check for app updates in the app store. Update or reinstall problematic apps.

14. Mobile OS App Store Issues:

Issue: Users may encounter problems with the app store, such as unable to download or update apps.

Troubleshooting: Check internet connectivity. Clear app store cache or data. Restart the device and try again.

15. Mobile OS Accessibility Settings:

Issue: Users with accessibility needs may face challenges with certain OS features.

Troubleshooting: Configure accessibility settings according to user requirements. Use assistive technology if needed.

16. Mobile OS Keyboard and Input Problems:

Issue: The virtual keyboard or input methods may not function correctly.

Troubleshooting: Restart the device. Clear keyboard cache and data. Update keyboard app if available.

17. Mobile OS Camera and Multimedia Issues:

Issue: Problems with the device's camera, gallery, or multimedia playback.

Troubleshooting: Restart the device. Clear camera app cache and data. Update multimedia apps if available.

18. Mobile OS Location and GPS Troubles:

Issue: Location services and GPS may not work accurately.

Troubleshooting: Ensure location services are enabled. Restart the device. Update location-based apps.

19. Mobile OS Overheating:

Issue: Mobile devices may overheat during intensive usage.

Troubleshooting: Avoid using the device in direct sunlight or high-temperature environments. Close resource-intensive apps.

20. Mobile OS Screen Flickering or Display Issues:

Issue: The screen may flicker, display artifacts, or show abnormal colors.

Troubleshooting: Restart the device. Adjust display settings. Update graphics drivers if applicable.

21. Mobile OS Bluetooth and Connectivity Problems:

Issue: Bluetooth connections may drop or fail to establish.

Troubleshooting: Toggle Bluetooth off and on. Restart the device and Bluetooth devices. Ensure devices are within the Bluetooth range.

22. Mobile OS Multitasking and App Switching:

Issue: App switching and multitasking may not work as expected.

Troubleshooting: Restart the device. Check for app updates. Clear app cache and data.

23. Mobile OS Gaming and Performance Issues:

Issue: Mobile games may encounter lag or poor performance.

Troubleshooting: Close background apps. Adjust game settings for better performance.

24. Mobile OS Synchronization Problems:

Issue: Synchronization issues between mobile devices and cloud services.

Troubleshooting: Check internet connectivity. Verify account settings for synchronization.

25. Mobile OS VPN and Network Configuration:

Issue: VPN and network settings may cause connectivity issues.

Troubleshooting: Review VPN and network settings. Reset network settings if needed.

Quiz

1. **Question:** What is the primary function of the motherboard in a computer system?
   A. Execute software instructions
   B. Store data permanently
   C. Provide power to the components
   D. Connect and communicate between components

2. **Question:** What is the smallest unit of data in a computer?
   A. Bit
   B. Byte
   C. Kilobyte
   D. Megabyte

3. **Question:** Which component of the CPU performs arithmetic calculations?
   A. ALU (Arithmetic Logic Unit)
   B. Control Unit
   C. Cache Memory
   D. Registers

4. **Question:** Which type of storage is non-volatile and retains data even when the power is off?
   A. RAM (Random Access Memory)
   B. Cache Memory
   C. SSD (Solid State Drive)
   D. HDD (Hard Disk Drive)

5. **Question:** What does BIOS stand for in the context of a computer system?
   A. Basic Input Output System
   B. Basic Integrated Operating System
   C. Binary Input Output Service
   D. Binary Integrated Operating Service

6. **Question:** Which storage device is typically used to store the operating system and software applications in a computer system?
   A. RAM (Random Access Memory)
   B. HDD (Hard Disk Drive)
   C. CPU (Central Processing Unit)
   D. SSD (Solid State Drive)

7. **Question:** Which peripheral device is used to input text and commands into a computer?

    A. Monitor
    B. Keyboard
    C. Printer
    D. Scanner

8. **Question:** Which component of a computer system is responsible for executing instructions of a computer program?

    A. RAM (Random Access Memory)
    B. CPU (Central Processing Unit)
    C. Motherboard
    D. Power Supply Unit

9. **Question:** Which type of network is used to connect devices within a limited geographic area, like an office or home?

    A. LAN (Local Area Network)
    B. WAN (Wide Area Network)
    C. MAN (Metropolitan Area Network)
    D. PAN (Personal Area Network)

10. **Question:** Which network device is used to connect multiple devices in a network and forward data packets between them?

    A. Modem
    B. Router
    C. Hub
    D. Switch

11. **Question:** Which network protocol is commonly used to retrieve email messages from a mail server?

    A. HTTP (Hypertext Transfer Protocol)
    B. SMTP (Simple Mail Transfer Protocol)
    C. FTP (File Transfer Protocol)
    D. POP3 (Post Office Protocol version 3)

12. **Question:** Which network technology allows devices to communicate with each other over short distances without using cables?

    A. Ethernet
    B. Bluetooth

C. Wi-Fi

D. Fiber Optic

13. **Question:** Which component of a mobile device is responsible for processing data and running applications?

   A. Battery

   B. RAM (Random Access Memory)

   C. CPU (Central Processing Unit)

   D. Touchscreen

14. **Question:** Which mobile operating system is developed by Apple Inc.?

   A. Android

   B. iOS

   C. Windows Mobile

   D. Linux

15. **Question:** Which mobile OS feature allows users to unlock the device using their fingerprint or face?

   A. Face ID

   B. Touch ID

   C. Face Unlock

   D. Fingerprint Unlock

16. **Question:** What is the process of removing unnecessary files and programs to free up storage space and improve performance called on mobile devices?

   A. Defragmentation

   B. Disk Cleanup

   C. Cache Clearing

   D. Factory Reset

17. **Question:** Which mobile OS allows users to customize their home screen with widgets and app icons?

   A. Android

   B. iOS

   C. Windows Mobile

   D. BlackBerry OS

Operational Procedures

The Operational Procedures chapter covers essential practices and protocols for effectively managing and maintaining computer systems and networks. It includes topics related to documentation, disaster recovery, backup procedures, user training, and security protocols. Let's explore some key topics in this chapter:

1. **Documentation Best Practices:**

Importance of documentation: Explain the significance of maintaining detailed records of system configurations, changes, and troubleshooting steps.

Documentation types: Describe different types of documentation, such as network diagrams, hardware and software inventories, and standard operating procedures (SOPs).

2. **Change Management:**

Change control process: Outline the steps involved in implementing changes to a system or network while minimizing potential risks and disruptions.

Change approval and authorization: Explain the need for formal approval and authorization before implementing changes.

3. **Disaster Recovery Planning:**

Disaster recovery goals: Define the objectives of disaster recovery planning, including minimizing downtime and data loss.

Disaster recovery strategies: Describe various recovery strategies, such as backup and restore, hot and cold sites, and cloud-based solutions.

4. **Backup and Recovery Procedures:**

Backup types: Discuss different backup types, such as full, incremental, and differential backups.

Backup schedules: Explain the importance of establishing regular backup schedules and testing backup integrity.

5. **User Training and Support:**

Training programs: Address the need for comprehensive user training to ensure efficient system usage and reduce user-related issues.

Helpdesk support: Describe the role of a helpdesk in assisting users with technical issues and inquiries.

6. **Security Awareness and Training:**

Security policies: Emphasize the importance of implementing and enforcing security policies to protect sensitive data and systems.

Security training: Explain the need for ongoing security training to educate users about potential threats and best security practices.

7. **Incident Response and Handling:**

Incident categories: Classify and prioritize different types of incidents based on severity and impact.

Incident response procedures: Outline the steps for identifying, reporting, and resolving security incidents.

8. **Compliance and Legal Considerations:**

Regulatory requirements: Address compliance with relevant industry standards and government regulations.

Data privacy: Explain the significance of protecting user data and ensuring compliance with data privacy laws.

9. **Ethical Considerations:**

Ethical usage of technology: Discuss the ethical responsibilities of IT professionals, including respecting user privacy and intellectual property.

10. **Environmental Controls:**

Temperature and humidity management: Describe the importance of maintaining appropriate environmental conditions for hardware.

11. **Hardware and Software Life Cycle Management:**

Hardware refresh cycles: Explain the need for periodic hardware upgrades and replacements.

Software updates and patches: Emphasize the significance of keeping software up-to-date with the latest security patches.

12. **Network Maintenance and Monitoring:**

Regular network maintenance: Describe the importance of regular network checks, updates, and performance monitoring.

Network monitoring tools: Introduce various network monitoring tools used to identify and resolve network issues proactively.

13. Inventory Management:

Hardware and software inventory: Emphasize the need for maintaining up-to-date records of all hardware and software assets.

License compliance: Explain the importance of ensuring that software licenses are valid and compliant with the terms of use.

14. IT Service Management (ITSM):

IT service catalog: Describe the concept of an IT service catalog that outlines available services for users.

Service level agreements (SLAs): Explain the use of SLAs to define service expectations and performance metrics.

15. Capacity Planning:

Resource utilization monitoring: Discuss the practice of monitoring resource usage to predict future capacity needs.

Scalability considerations: Address the importance of planning for the system's ability to handle increased workloads.

16. Virtualization and Cloud Computing:

Virtual machine management: Explain the benefits and challenges of managing virtualized environments.

Cloud deployment models: Introduce public, private, and hybrid cloud deployment options.

17. Remote Access and VPNs:

Remote access security: Address security considerations when allowing remote access to the network.

VPN (Virtual Private Network): Explain the use of VPNs to create secure connections for remote users.

18. Asset Disposal and E-waste Management:

Safe disposal of assets: Describe the proper disposal methods for retired hardware and data sanitization.

E-waste recycling: Address the environmental impact of electronic waste and the importance of responsible recycling.

19. Business Continuity Planning:

Continuity planning process: Outline the steps involved in creating a business continuity plan to ensure operations during disruptions.

Testing and validation: Discuss the need for regular testing and validation of business continuity plans.

20. Outsourcing and Vendor Management:

Vendor selection: Address factors to consider when selecting and partnering with IT service providers.

Service level agreements (SLAs): Explain the use of SLAs to define expectations and hold vendors accountable.

21. End-User Policies and Acceptable Use:

Acceptable use policy (AUP): Introduce policies that define acceptable usage of IT resources by end-users.

Social media and internet usage: Address guidelines for appropriate use of social media and internet resources.

22. Data Backup and Recovery Testing:

Backup testing procedures: Describe the importance of regularly testing backups to ensure data recoverability.

Disaster recovery drills: Explain the need for periodic disaster recovery drills to evaluate response readiness.

23. Root Cause Analysis:

Problem-solving process: Outline the steps involved in identifying and addressing the root cause of IT issues.

Preventive measures: Emphasize the importance of implementing preventive measures to avoid recurrent problems.

24. Incident Reporting and Documentation:

Incident reporting procedures: Explain the process of reporting incidents accurately and promptly.

Incident documentation: Address the need for detailed incident documentation for analysis and future reference.

25. Data Classification and Security:

Data classification levels: Describe the classification of data based on sensitivity and confidentiality.

Data security controls: Address security measures to protect data based on its classification.

26. Remote Support and Troubleshooting:

Remote support tools: Introduce tools used for remote troubleshooting and problem resolution.

Secure remote access: Emphasize the importance of secure remote access to protect data and systems.

27. Physical Security Measures:

Access control: Describe measures to control physical access to IT infrastructure and facilities.

Video surveillance: Address the use of video surveillance for security monitoring.

28. Security Incident Response Team (SIRT):

SIRT roles and responsibilities: Describe the roles and responsibilities of the Security Incident Response Team.

Incident response plan: Explain the creation and implementation of an incident response plan.

29. Data Backup and Recovery Procedures:

Backup verification: Emphasize the need to verify backups for data integrity and completeness.

Recovery testing: Describe the process of testing data recovery to ensure successful restoration.

30. Network Access Control (NAC):

NAC implementation: Explain how NAC can be used to control access to the network based on device health and user credentials.

Guest network access: Address considerations for providing guest access to the network securely.

9.1 Environmental Controls

Environmental controls are measures taken to maintain the optimal physical conditions required for the proper functioning and longevity of computer systems and network infrastructure. These controls help prevent hardware failures, reduce energy consumption, and ensure a stable working environment for IT equipment. Here are some key aspects of environmental controls:

1. **Temperature Management:**

Temperature range: Maintain a controlled temperature range, typically between 20 to 25 degrees Celsius (68 to 77 degrees Fahrenheit), to prevent overheating or equipment damage.

Cooling systems: Use air conditioning or cooling solutions like fans to dissipate heat generated by computer equipment.

2. **Humidity Control:**

Optimal humidity level: Maintain humidity levels between 40% to 60% to prevent static electricity buildup and reduce the risk of equipment damage.

Dehumidifiers: Use dehumidifiers in areas with high humidity to control moisture levels.

3. **Air Quality:**

Air filtration: Install air filters to remove dust and particles from the air, which can accumulate on sensitive hardware components.

Clean environment: Keep the IT equipment room clean and free from debris to avoid clogging vents and airflow paths.

4. **Ventilation:**

Proper airflow: Ensure that computer equipment has adequate space around it to facilitate proper airflow and cooling.

Cable management: Organize and manage cables to prevent obstruction of airflow and reduce clutter.

5. **Power Management:**

Uninterruptible Power Supply (UPS): Install UPS devices to provide backup power in case of power outages and prevent data loss or hardware damage.

Power monitoring: Monitor power consumption to optimize energy efficiency and identify potential issues.

6. Noise Reduction:

Noise control: Minimize noise levels in IT equipment rooms to create a comfortable working environment for personnel and avoid disturbances.

7. Fire Suppression:

Fire extinguishing systems: Implement fire suppression systems, such as fire extinguishers or automatic sprinklers, to protect equipment from fire-related damage.

Smoke detection: Install smoke detectors to detect early signs of fire and trigger appropriate responses.

8. Physical Security:

Access control: Restrict access to IT equipment rooms to authorized personnel only to prevent unauthorized tampering or theft.

Security cameras: Deploy security cameras to monitor the IT environment and deter potential security breaches.

9. E-waste Management:

Responsible disposal: Ensure proper disposal of retired or obsolete IT equipment to minimize environmental impact and comply with e-waste regulations.

Recycling programs: Participate in recycling programs to recycle electronic waste in an eco-friendly manner.

10. Environmental Monitoring:

Monitoring systems: Use environmental monitoring systems to continuously track temperature, humidity, and other environmental factors in the IT environment.

Alert notifications: Set up alert notifications to promptly respond to any critical environmental changes or equipment failures.

11. Redundancy Planning:

Redundant systems: Implement redundant cooling and power systems to ensure continuity in case of primary system failures.

Failover mechanisms: Establish failover mechanisms for critical components to provide seamless operations during hardware failures.

12. Temperature and Humidity Monitoring:

Automated monitoring: Utilize automated systems to monitor temperature and humidity levels continuously and receive alerts in case of deviations from the optimal range.

Remote monitoring: Implement remote monitoring capabilities to access environmental data from anywhere, facilitating quick response to critical conditions.

13. Cooling Solutions:

Precision cooling: Consider using precision cooling solutions like computer room air conditioners (CRAC) or computer room air handlers (CRAH) to maintain precise temperature control.

Hot aisle/cold aisle configuration: Organize server racks in a hot aisle/cold aisle configuration to optimize cooling efficiency and prevent hot air recirculation.

14. Energy Efficiency:

Energy-efficient hardware: Invest in energy-efficient servers, switches, and other network equipment to reduce power consumption and operational costs.

Virtualization: Utilize server virtualization to consolidate multiple physical servers into a single host, improving energy efficiency and reducing hardware footprint.

15. Disaster Preparedness:

Backup power sources: Establish backup power sources like generators or redundant power feeds to ensure continuous operation during prolonged power outages.

Disaster recovery plans: Develop and test disaster recovery plans to mitigate the impact of environmental disasters like floods or earthquakes.

16. Remote Monitoring and Management:

Remote access solutions: Deploy remote access tools to manage and troubleshoot IT infrastructure from a centralized location.

Automated responses: Implement automated responses to environmental alerts to initiate corrective actions without manual intervention.

17. Cable Management:

Organized cable routing: Properly route and manage cables to avoid obstructing airflow and reduce the risk of accidental disconnections.

Cable labeling: Label cables to facilitate identification and maintenance tasks, reducing the likelihood of errors during troubleshooting.

18. Physical Access Controls:

Biometric access: Consider using biometric access control systems for an added layer of security and to prevent unauthorized access.

Visitor policies: Implement visitor policies to ensure visitors are accompanied and supervised while accessing critical IT areas.

19. Regular Maintenance:

Cleaning schedules: Establish regular cleaning schedules for IT equipment, including fans, filters, and server racks, to remove dust and debris.

Preventive maintenance: Conduct preventive maintenance checks on cooling systems, power supplies, and other critical components to identify potential issues before they become problems.

20. Environmental Compliance:

Regulatory requirements: Comply with environmental regulations and guidelines related to IT infrastructure and electronic waste management.

Green certifications: Seek green certifications for data centers and IT facilities to demonstrate commitment to environmental responsibility.

21. Training and Awareness:

Environmental awareness training: Educate IT personnel about the importance of environmental controls and their roles in maintaining a conducive IT environment.

Environmental policy: Establish and communicate an environmental policy outlining the organization's commitment to environmental sustainability.

9.2 Safety Procedures and Policies

Safety procedures and policies are essential in any IT environment to protect the well-being of personnel, prevent accidents, and maintain a safe working environment. These procedures and policies encompass a wide range of practices aimed at mitigating risks associated with IT equipment, electrical systems, and physical surroundings. Here are some key safety procedures and policies:

1. **Electrical Safety:**

Electrical hazards: Educate personnel about the dangers of electric shocks, electrical fires, and short circuits.

Proper grounding: Ensure all IT equipment is properly grounded to prevent electrical hazards.

2. **Fire Safety:**

Fire prevention: Implement fire prevention measures, such as regular inspection of electrical systems and avoidance of overloading power outlets.

Fire extinguishers: Provide easily accessible fire extinguishers and conduct training on their proper usage.

3. **Emergency Evacuation:**

Emergency procedures: Establish clear emergency evacuation procedures and conduct regular drills to familiarize personnel with evacuation routes.

Emergency exits: Ensure that emergency exits are clearly marked and unobstructed at all times.

4. **First Aid and Medical Support:**

First aid kits: Keep well-stocked first aid kits in IT areas to address minor injuries promptly.

Medical support: Establish protocols for seeking medical assistance in case of more serious incidents.

5. **Ergonomics and Workspace Safety:**

Ergonomic workstations: Set up workstations ergonomically to prevent injuries such as back strain, carpal tunnel syndrome, and eye strain.

Workstation cleanliness: Encourage regular cleaning and disinfection of workstations to maintain a hygienic environment.

6. **Chemical Safety:**

Hazardous materials: Ensure proper handling and storage of any chemicals used in IT environments.

Material Safety Data Sheets (MSDS): Maintain MSDS for all chemicals and make them accessible to personnel.

7. Lifting and Moving Equipment:

Safe lifting techniques: Train personnel on safe lifting techniques to avoid back injuries when handling heavy equipment.

Equipment moving procedures: Use proper tools and equipment when moving heavy IT equipment.

8. Security Awareness:

Physical security: Educate personnel about the importance of maintaining physical security measures, such as locking doors and securing equipment.

Social engineering: Raise awareness about social engineering attacks and the importance of not divulging sensitive information.

9. Hazardous Waste Disposal:

Proper disposal: Adhere to regulations for disposing of hazardous waste, such as batteries and electronic components, in an environmentally responsible manner.

Recycling programs: Encourage participation in electronic waste recycling programs to minimize environmental impact.

10. Personal Protective Equipment (PPE):

PPE requirements: Identify appropriate PPE, such as safety glasses or gloves, for specific tasks that involve potential hazards.

PPE training: Provide training on the proper use and care of PPE to ensure maximum effectiveness.

11. Access Control and Visitor Policies:

Restricted access: Limit access to IT areas to authorized personnel only to prevent unauthorized tampering or accidents.

Visitor guidelines: Enforce visitor policies, including sign-in procedures and escorts, to monitor and manage access.

12. Electrical Equipment Inspection:

Regular inspections: Conduct regular inspections of electrical equipment, power cords, and outlets to identify potential hazards or wear.

Defective equipment handling: Establish protocols for reporting and removing defective electrical equipment from service.

13. Prohibited Practices:

Smoking restrictions: Enforce no-smoking policies in IT areas to prevent fire hazards.

Food and drink restrictions: Prohibit the consumption of food and beverages near sensitive IT equipment to prevent spills and contamination.

14. Chemical Spill Response:

Spill containment: Provide spill containment materials and train personnel on proper chemical spill response procedures.

Safety showers and eye wash stations: Ensure access to safety showers and eye wash stations in case of chemical spills.

15. Equipment Safety Labels:

Warning labels: Affix warning labels on potentially hazardous equipment to alert personnel of specific risks and precautions.

16. Regular Safety Training:

Mandatory safety training: Require all personnel to undergo regular safety training sessions to reinforce safety procedures and policies.

Training records: Maintain records of safety training sessions attended by each employee.

17. Reporting Safety Concerns:

Open communication: Encourage personnel to report safety concerns, hazards, or near-miss incidents promptly.

Safety reporting procedures: Establish a clear process for reporting safety issues to the appropriate authorities.

18. Lockout/Tagout (LOTO):

Equipment isolation: Implement LOTO procedures when servicing or repairing equipment to prevent accidental energization.

Lockout devices and tags: Provide appropriate lockout devices and tags for authorized personnel.

19. Security Cameras and Alarms:

Surveillance: Utilize security cameras to monitor critical areas and deter potential intruders.

Intrusion alarms: Install intrusion detection alarms to notify personnel of unauthorized access.

20. Heat and Noise Management:

Heat dissipation: Implement measures to dissipate heat generated by IT equipment to prevent overheating.

Noise reduction: Address excessive noise levels in IT areas to ensure a comfortable and productive work environment.

21. Safe Equipment Storage:

Secure storage: Store spare equipment and hazardous materials in designated secure storage areas.

Rack stability: Ensure proper installation and anchoring of server racks to prevent accidental tipping.

22. Fire Drills and Emergency Preparedness:

Fire drills: Conduct periodic fire drills to familiarize personnel with evacuation procedures and emergency exits.

Emergency response teams: Designate and train emergency response teams to handle specific types of incidents, such as fires or chemical spills.

23. Safety Inspections and Audits:

Regular inspections: Perform routine safety inspections to identify potential hazards and ensure compliance with safety policies.

Third-party audits: Consider third-party safety audits to gain an objective evaluation of safety practices.

24. Safety Signage and Visual Cues:

Warning signs: Install safety signs to warn personnel of potential dangers, such as high-voltage areas or restricted access zones.

Floor markings: Use floor markings to indicate safe walkways and emergency exit routes.

25. Safe Handling of Chemicals and Hazardous Materials:

Material handling guidelines: Educate personnel on safe procedures for handling, storing, and disposing of hazardous chemicals and materials.

Personal protective equipment (PPE): Require the use of appropriate PPE when handling hazardous substances.

26. Safety Protocols for Data Centers:

Data center access control: Implement strict access controls to data centers, allowing entry only to authorized personnel.

Data center environment monitoring: Install environmental monitoring systems to detect any anomalies that may affect IT equipment.

27. Crisis Communication Plan:

Communication channels: Establish communication channels for crisis situations, ensuring that employees can receive critical updates promptly.

Contact lists: Maintain updated contact lists for key personnel and emergency services.

28. Equipment Maintenance and Safety Checks:

Regular maintenance: Schedule regular maintenance checks for IT equipment and infrastructure to identify and address safety concerns.

Safety inspections: Conduct safety inspections to verify that equipment is in proper working condition and compliant with safety standards.

29. Safe Handling of IT Hardware:

Safe lifting and transport: Train personnel on proper techniques for lifting and transporting IT hardware to prevent injuries.

Equipment disposal: Follow proper procedures for disposing of IT hardware, particularly for devices containing hazardous materials.

30. Personal Safety and Health Guidelines:

Personal hygiene: Encourage personal hygiene practices to prevent the spread of illnesses in the workplace.

Injury reporting: Establish procedures for reporting and addressing work-related injuries promptly.

9.3 Communication and Professionalism

Effective communication and professionalism are essential skills for IT professionals to succeed in their roles and collaborate with others in the workplace. Good communication fosters a positive work environment, enhances teamwork, and ensures that IT projects are successful. Here are some key aspects of communication and professionalism in the IT field:

1. **Clear and Concise Communication:**

Email etiquette: Use clear and professional language in emails, ensuring proper grammar and punctuation.

Avoid jargon: Explain technical concepts in simple terms when communicating with non-technical stakeholders.

2. **Active Listening:**

Pay attention: Give full attention when others are speaking, and avoid interrupting.

Clarify understanding: Ask questions to ensure you understand the message accurately.

3. **Respectful and Courteous Behavior:**

Treat others with respect: Be polite and considerate to colleagues, clients, and end-users.

Conflict resolution: Address conflicts professionally and strive to find mutually beneficial solutions.

4. **Effective Team Collaboration:**

Share knowledge: Collaborate with team members by sharing ideas, expertise, and best practices.

Constructive feedback: Provide feedback in a constructive and respectful manner.

5. **Professional Appearance:**

Dress code: Adhere to the organization's dress code policy and present a professional appearance.

Virtual professionalism: Maintain professionalism in virtual meetings and video conferences.

6. **Time Management:**

Prioritize tasks: Organize and prioritize tasks to meet deadlines and manage workload effectively.

Promptness: Be punctual for meetings, appointments, and project deliverables.

7. **Documentation Skills:**

Thorough documentation: Maintain detailed and accurate documentation of IT processes, procedures, and projects.

Version control: Use version control systems for tracking changes to documentation and code.

8. Customer Service:

Empathy: Show empathy and understanding when assisting end-users with technical issues.

Patience: Be patient and avoid frustration when dealing with users who may have limited technical knowledge.

9. Presentation Skills:

Effective presentations: Deliver clear and engaging presentations to technical and non-technical audiences.

Visual aids: Use visual aids like slides and diagrams to enhance presentations.

10. Conflict Resolution:

Stay composed: Remain calm and composed during challenging situations or conflicts.

Mediation: Offer to mediate conflicts between team members to facilitate resolution.

11. Ethics and Integrity:

Honesty: Always act with honesty and integrity, especially when handling sensitive data and confidential information.

Code of conduct: Adhere to the organization's code of conduct and ethical guidelines.

12. Adaptability and Flexibility:

Adapt to change: Embrace change and be open to new technologies and methodologies.

Handling uncertainty: Remain composed and adapt quickly in fast-paced or uncertain situations.

13. Problem-Solving and Critical Thinking:

Analytical approach: Apply critical thinking skills to analyze and solve complex IT problems.

Resourcefulness: Demonstrate resourcefulness in finding solutions to technical challenges.

14. Professional Development:

Continuous learning: Pursue ongoing professional development to stay updated with the latest IT trends and technologies.

Certifications: Obtain relevant certifications to showcase expertise and commitment to professional growth.

15. Confidentiality and Data Protection:

Data privacy: Respect and protect the privacy of users' data and sensitive information.

Access controls: Implement access controls to prevent unauthorized access to confidential data.

16. Cross-Cultural Communication:

Cultural sensitivity: Be mindful of cultural differences when communicating with colleagues and clients from diverse backgrounds.

Language barriers: Adapt communication to accommodate language differences.

17. Positive Attitude:

Optimism: Maintain a positive and optimistic attitude, even in challenging situations.

Motivation: Stay motivated and enthusiastic about IT projects and tasks.

18. Team Building:

Collaboration activities: Participate in team-building activities to strengthen relationships and foster camaraderie.

Recognize achievements: Acknowledge and celebrate team members' accomplishments.

19. Conflict-Free Communication:

Avoid gossip: Refrain from participating in workplace gossip or spreading rumors.

Clear communication channels: Encourage open and transparent communication to prevent misunderstandings.

20. Empowerment and Delegation:

Delegate tasks: Delegate responsibilities to team members based on their strengths and expertise.

Encourage innovation: Empower team members to contribute innovative ideas and solutions.

21. Negotiation Skills:

Win-win approach: Use a collaborative approach to negotiate win-win solutions in project discussions or contract negotiations.

Compromise: Be willing to compromise when necessary to achieve mutually beneficial outcomes.

22. Stress Management:

Stress reduction techniques: Practice stress-reducing techniques, such as mindfulness and time management, to maintain a healthy work-life balance.

Seek support: Reach out for support from colleagues or supervisors when feeling overwhelmed.

23. Communication in Crisis Situations:

Crisis communication plan: Be prepared to communicate effectively during crisis situations, providing timely updates to relevant stakeholders.

Transparency: Maintain transparency and honesty in communication during challenging times.

24. Networking and Relationship Building:

Professional networking: Build and maintain professional relationships within the IT industry to stay connected and updated with industry trends.

Community involvement: Participate in IT-related communities and events to expand professional networks.

25. Collaboration with Non-Technical Stakeholders:

Adapt communication style: Tailor communication to suit the technical understanding of non-technical stakeholders.

Translate technical terms: Explain technical concepts in layman's terms to ensure clear understanding.

26. Conflict-Free Communication:

Active listening: Listen actively to understand others' perspectives before responding.

Avoid assumptions: Avoid making assumptions and seek clarifications when necessary to prevent misunderstandings.

Feedback and Constructive Criticism:

27. **Giving feedback:** Provide constructive feedback to colleagues and team members in a professional and supportive manner.

Receiving feedback: Accept feedback graciously and use it as an opportunity for growth and improvement.

28. Social Media and Online Presence:

Professional conduct: Maintain a professional online presence and be mindful of how social media activity reflects on the organization.

Avoid controversy: Refrain from engaging in controversial discussions or making divisive statements on social media.

29. Diplomacy and Tactfulness:

Diplomatic communication: Handle sensitive or difficult conversations with diplomacy and tact.

Conflict de-escalation: Use diplomatic approaches to de-escalate conflicts and find resolutions.

30. Customer-Centric Approach:

Customer-focused mindset: Keep the needs and satisfaction of end-users and customers at the forefront of IT solutions and services.

User feedback: Seek feedback from end-users to continuously improve IT services and support.

31. Cultural Competence:

Understanding diversity: Be aware of cultural differences and adapt communication styles to be inclusive and respectful.

Cultural sensitivity training: Participate in training sessions that promote cultural competence in the workplace.

32. Conflict Management:

Constructive resolution: Address conflicts promptly and constructively to prevent escalation and maintain a positive work environment.

Mediation skills: Develop mediation skills to help resolve conflicts between team members or departments.

33. Accountability:

Ownership of tasks: Take responsibility for assigned tasks and deliverables, meeting deadlines and quality standards.

Admitting mistakes: Be willing to admit mistakes and take corrective actions when necessary.

34. Remote Communication Skills:

Effective virtual communication: Master virtual communication tools, such as video conferencing and collaboration platforms.

Clear written communication: Articulate ideas clearly in written messages, as remote communication relies heavily on written exchanges.

35. Time and Meeting Management:

Productive meetings: Conduct efficient meetings with clear agendas, time management, and action items.

Scheduling considerations: Respect colleagues' time and availability when scheduling meetings and appointments.

36. Conflict Resolution Training:

Training programs: Participate in conflict resolution workshops to develop effective conflict resolution techniques.

Role-playing exercises: Practice conflict resolution scenarios through role-playing exercises.

37. Presentation Confidence:

Public speaking skills: Build confidence in public speaking and delivering presentations to both technical and non-technical audiences.

Engaging delivery: Deliver presentations with enthusiasm and engage the audience with compelling content.

38. Empathy in Customer Interactions:

Understanding end-users: Empathize with end-users' frustrations and challenges, showing understanding and support.

Patient assistance: Offer patient and empathetic assistance during IT support interactions.

39. Professional Email Communication:

Formal language: Use a formal tone and proper salutations in professional emails.

Reply promptly: Respond to emails in a timely manner to maintain effective communication.

40. Conflict De-Escalation Techniques:

Emotional intelligence: Develop emotional intelligence to recognize and manage emotions during conflict situations.

Remain calm: Stay composed and avoid escalating conflicts further during discussions.

41. Mentoring and Knowledge Sharing:

Mentorship programs: Engage in mentoring relationships to share knowledge and experience with less experienced colleagues.

Knowledge sharing sessions: Participate in knowledge-sharing sessions to promote a culture of continuous learning.

42. Networking and Relationship Maintenance:

Professional events: Attend conferences, seminars, and networking events to expand professional connections.

Follow-up: Follow up with contacts made at networking events to nurture professional relationships.

43. Conflict Resolution Documentation:

Incident reports: Document conflict resolution efforts and outcomes for reference and improvement.

Lessons learned: Record lessons learned from conflict resolution experiences for future use.

44. Remote Collaboration Tools:

Collaboration platforms: Familiarize yourself with remote collaboration tools, such as project management software and shared document platforms.

Virtual team communication: Use virtual team communication channels effectively to stay connected and updated.

45. Career Development Planning:

Goal setting: Set professional development goals and create a plan for achieving them.

Skill gap analysis: Identify skill gaps and seek opportunities to acquire missing skills.

46. Non-Verbal Communication:

Body language: Be mindful of your body language in both face-to-face and virtual interactions.

Eye contact: Maintain appropriate eye contact during conversations to convey attentiveness.

47. Conflict Resolution Mediation:

Mediation techniques: Learn and apply mediation techniques to facilitate productive conflict resolution discussions.

Neutral approach: Maintain a neutral and impartial stance during conflict mediation.

48. Online Collaboration Etiquette:

Virtual meeting etiquette: Follow virtual meeting etiquette, such as muting microphones when not speaking and avoiding interruptions.

Email response time: Respond to emails promptly, even when working remotely.

49. Managing Workload and Priorities:

Task organization: Use task management tools to prioritize and manage your workload efficiently.

Time-blocking: Allocate specific time blocks for different tasks to maintain focus and avoid multitasking.

50. IT Support Service Excellence:

Customer feedback: Seek feedback from end-users to gauge IT support service quality and identify areas for improvement.

Service improvement plans: Implement improvement plans based on customer feedback and support data analysis.

Quiz

1. What is the primary function of the CPU in a computer?
    a) Execute instructions
    b) Store data
    c) Provide power
    d) Connect to the internet

2. Which type of storage device is typically the fastest but also the most expensive?
    a) Hard Disk Drive (HDD)
    b) Solid State Drive (SSD)
    c) USB Flash Drive
    d) CD-ROM

3. Which component of the computer is responsible for storing the operating system, programs, and user data permanently?
    a) RAM
    b) CPU
    c) Hard Disk Drive (HDD)
    d) Motherboard

4. What does BIOS stand for in a computer system?
    a) Basic Input Output System
    b) Binary Input Output System
    c) Basic Internal Operating System
    d) Bootable Input Output Software

5. Which of the following is NOT an example of a peripheral device?
    a) Monitor
    b) Keyboard
    c) CPU
    d) Printer

6. Which type of network topology uses a central hub or switch to connect all devices?
    a) Bus
    b) Star
    c) Ring
    d) Mesh

7. What network protocol is commonly used for sending emails?

a) HTTP

b) SMTP

c) FTP

d) DNS

8. Which cable type is typically used to connect computers to a Local Area Network (LAN)?

    a) HDMI

    b) USB

    c) Ethernet

    d) VGA

9. What does DHCP stand for in networking?

    a) Domain Hosting Configuration Protocol

    b) Dynamic Host Configuration Protocol

    c) Digital Hosting Control Protocol

    d) Distributed Host Configuration Provider

10. Which of the following is a wireless communication technology commonly used in smartphones and other mobile devices?

    a) LAN

    b) Wi-Fi

    c) Ethernet

    d) Bluetooth

11. Which mobile operating system is developed by Apple Inc.?

    a) Android

    b) iOS

    c) Windows Mobile

    d) BlackBerry OS

12. What is the purpose of a firewall in network security?

    a) To block internet access

    b) To prevent physical intrusions

    c) To monitor network traffic and block unauthorized access

    d) To encrypt data transmissions

13. What is the term used to describe malicious software that disguises itself as legitimate software to gain unauthorized access to a computer system?

    a) Firewall

b) Spyware

c) Phishing

d) Trojan horse

14. Which security measure involves the use of multiple authentication factors, such as a password and a fingerprint scan, to verify a user's identity?

    a) Encryption

    b) Biometrics

    c) Firewall

    d) Antivirus

15. Which of the following is an example of a physical security measure?

    a) Strong passwords

    b) Data encryption

    c) Security cameras

    d) Intrusion detection software

16. Which step is typically the first in the troubleshooting process?

    a) Implement the solution

    b) Identify the problem

    c) Test the solution

    d) Document the problem

17. Which component of a computer system is responsible for executing software instructions and performing calculations?

    a) Motherboard

    b) CPU (Central Processing Unit)

    c) RAM (Random Access Memory)

    d) Power Supply Unit (PSU)

18. RAID stands for:

    a) Redundant Array of Independent Disks

    b) Random Access Information Drive

    c) Remote Access Intrusion Detection

    d) Rapid Application Installation and Deployment

19. Which network topology connects each device in a closed loop, forming a circular path for data transmission?

    a) Star

b) Bus

c) Ring

d) Mesh

20. Which network protocol is used for transferring files over the internet?

a) HTTP

b) FTP (File Transfer Protocol)

c) SMTP

d) TCP/IP

21. What type of storage device uses magnetic storage to store data and is commonly found in traditional desktop computers?

a) Solid State Drive (SSD)

b) Hard Disk Drive (HDD)

c) USB Flash Drive

d) CD-ROM

22. What is the purpose of the BIOS in a computer system?

a) To control the flow of data between the CPU and RAM

b) To store the operating system

c) To control the computer's basic operations and perform hardware checks during startup

d) To provide power to the motherboard

23. Which of the following is an example of an input device?

a) Monitor

b) Printer

c) Keyboard

d) Speakers

24. Which network protocol is used for translating human-readable domain names into IP addresses?

a) HTTP

b) FTP

c) DNS (Domain Name System)

d) SMTP

25. What is the purpose of a UPS (Uninterruptible Power Supply) in a computer system?

a) To provide extra storage space for files

b) To regulate the flow of data between the CPU and RAM

c) To protect the computer from power outages and provide backup power

d) To connect the computer to the internet

26. Which mobile operating system is based on the Linux kernel and is open-source?

a) Android

b) iOS

c) Windows Mobile

d) BlackBerry OS

27. What is the primary function of an email client application?

a) To create and edit documents

b) To browse the internet

c) To send, receive, and manage email messages

d) To play multimedia files

28. What is the purpose of a router in a network?

a) To connect multiple networks together

b) To store data temporarily

c) To display web pages on a computer screen

d) To direct network traffic and forward data between different networks

29. What is the term used to describe the unauthorized access and manipulation of computer systems or data?

a) Hacking

b) Phishing

c) Spyware

d) Firewall

30. What type of software is designed to detect, prevent, and remove malicious software from a computer system?

a) Antivirus

b) Firewall

c) Encryption software

d) Spyware

Review and Exam Preparation

As we reach the end of this comprehensive guide, the "Review and Exam Preparation" chapter aims to help you consolidate your understanding of the topics covered and prepare for any assessments or exams related to computer systems, hardware, networking, mobile devices, operating systems, security, troubleshooting, and operational procedures. This chapter provides essential review materials and exam preparation strategies to ensure you're well-equipped to succeed.

10.1 Key Concepts Review:

Take time to review the key concepts, terminologies, and definitions presented in each chapter.

Summarize the main points and create study notes or flashcards to aid memorization.

10.2 Practice Quizzes:

Revisit the quizzes provided in each chapter to test your knowledge and identify areas that need further review.

Seek additional practice quizzes or exam-style questions to challenge yourself and reinforce your learning.

10.3 Hands-on Practice:

For topics related to hardware, networking, and troubleshooting, consider hands-on practice using a computer system.

Experiment with different configurations, set up a local network, or troubleshoot common hardware and software issues.

10.4 Exam Strategies:

Familiarize yourself with the exam format, duration, and types of questions you might encounter.

Time management: During the exam, allocate sufficient time for each section or question, and don't get stuck on challenging items.

10.5 Study Groups:

Form or join study groups with fellow learners to discuss and review topics collaboratively.

Explain concepts to others to reinforce your understanding.

10.6 Revision Plan:

Develop a comprehensive revision plan, allocating specific time to review each topic and chapter.

Set realistic goals and track your progress.

10.7 Seek Help and Clarifications:

Don't hesitate to seek help from instructors, mentors, or online resources if you encounter difficulties with certain concepts.

Address any misunderstandings to avoid confusion during exams.

10.8 Mock Exams:

Take advantage of mock exams or sample tests available online to simulate the exam environment and evaluate your readiness.

Analyze your performance to identify areas for improvement.

10.9 Stay Relaxed and Healthy:

Prioritize self-care during your exam preparation, including sufficient rest, balanced nutrition, and exercise.

Stay positive and confident in your abilities.

10.10 Additional Resources:

Explore supplementary resources such as online tutorials, video lectures, and educational websites to gain a deeper understanding of specific topics.

Utilize textbooks, online articles, and academic papers for in-depth study.

10.11 Time Management:

Create a study schedule that balances your exam preparation with other responsibilities and commitments.

Allocate more time to challenging topics while reviewing familiar concepts efficiently.

10.12 Hands-on Simulations:

Look for virtual labs and simulations that allow you to practice hands-on tasks related to computer systems, networking, and troubleshooting.

Simulations provide practical experience without the risk of damaging physical equipment.

10.13 Revision and Review Sessions:

Organize regular revision and review sessions to refresh your memory and reinforce key concepts.

Utilize mind maps or concept maps to visualize relationships between different topics.

10.14 Analyze Past Exams:

If past exams or sample questions are available, review them to identify recurring themes or patterns.

Focus on areas that are frequently assessed.

10.15 Seek Feedback:

Seek feedback from instructors, tutors, or study partners on your answers to practice questions or mock exams.

Use feedback to improve your approach to answering questions effectively.

10.16 Stay Motivated:

Set achievable milestones and reward yourself when you achieve them to maintain motivation during your exam preparation.

Visualize your success and the benefits of mastering the subject matter.

10.17 Reduce Distractions:

Minimize distractions during study sessions by creating a dedicated and quiet study environment.

Turn off notifications on your devices to stay focused.

10.18 Review Common Mistakes:

Analyze any mistakes made during practice exams or quizzes to understand the underlying reasons.

Learn from these mistakes to avoid repeating them in the actual exam.

10.19 Stay Positive and Confident:

Approach the exam with a positive mindset, believing in your preparation and abilities.

Manage test anxiety by practicing relaxation techniques before and during the exam.

10.20 Final Review:

Dedicate the final days before the exam to comprehensive review, emphasizing key concepts and core principles.

Avoid cramming and focus on understanding.

10.1 Review of Key Concepts

In this section, we will revisit the fundamental ideas and terminologies covered in the previous chapters related to computer systems, hardware, networking, mobile devices, operating systems, security, troubleshooting, and operational procedures. Use this review to reinforce your understanding of the core concepts.

1. Basic Computing Concepts

Computer: An electronic device that processes data according to a set of instructions (software) to perform tasks.

Hardware: The physical components of a computer system, including the CPU, RAM, motherboard, storage devices, etc.

Software: Programs and applications that control the computer's hardware and perform specific tasks.

Operating System: A software that manages computer hardware and provides an interface for users to interact with the computer.

2. Hardware

Motherboard: The main circuit board that connects all hardware components and provides communication between them.

CPU (Central Processing Unit): The "brain" of the computer that executes instructions and performs calculations.

RAM (Random Access Memory): Temporary memory that stores data and instructions needed by the CPU while the computer is running.

Storage Devices: Devices like HDD, SSD, and optical drives used to store data permanently.

Peripherals: External devices connected to the computer, such as keyboards, mice, printers, etc.

3. Networking

Network: A group of interconnected devices that can communicate and share resources.

LAN (Local Area Network): A network that covers a limited area, such as a home or office.

WAN (Wide Area Network): A network that covers a large geographical area, often spanning across cities or countries.

Router: A networking device that directs traffic between different networks.

4. Mobile Devices

Mobile OS: Operating systems designed for mobile devices, like Android and iOS.

Mobile Applications: Software designed to run on mobile devices, offering various functionalities.

Network Connectivity: The ability of mobile devices to connect to the internet via cellular data or Wi-Fi.

5. Troubleshooting

Troubleshooting Process: A systematic approach to identify and resolve issues in computer systems and networks.

Hardware Troubleshooting: Diagnosing and fixing hardware-related problems.

Software Troubleshooting: Diagnosing and fixing software-related issues.

6. Operating Systems

Windows OS: Microsoft's operating system for personal computers.

Linux: An open-source operating system commonly used in servers and other devices.

macOS: Apple's operating system for their computers.

7. Security

Physical Security: Measures to protect physical assets, like locks and security cameras.

Network Security: Measures to protect networks from unauthorized access and cyberattacks.

Computer Security Threats: Malware, phishing, and other threats that target computer systems and data.

8. Operational Procedures

Environmental Controls: Measures to maintain an optimal environment for computer systems, like temperature and humidity control.

Safety Procedures: Protocols to ensure the safety of individuals working with computer systems and equipment.

Communication and Professionalism: Effective communication and professionalism in the workplace.

9. Software Troubleshooting

Troubleshooting Microsoft Windows: Identifying and resolving common issues related to the Windows operating system.

Troubleshooting Other Operating Systems: Identifying and resolving common issues in non-Windows operating systems.

Troubleshooting Mobile OS: Identifying and resolving common issues in mobile operating systems like Android and iOS.

10. Review and Exam Preparation

Practice Quizzes: Taking practice quizzes to assess your knowledge and understanding of the topics covered.

Hands-on Practice: Engaging in hands-on activities and simulations to reinforce your learning.

Exam Strategies: Developing effective strategies to manage time and approach exam questions.

Study Groups: Collaborating with peers in study groups to discuss and review topics.

Revision Plan: Creating a structured plan to revise and review all chapters and topics systematically.

Additional Resources: Exploring supplementary resources like tutorials, articles, and textbooks for further learning.

11. Physical Security Measures

Access Control: Implementing measures to control physical access to secure areas.

Security Cameras: Installing surveillance cameras for monitoring and recording activities.

Alarms and Sensors: Using alarms and sensors to detect unauthorized entry or security breaches.

12. Network Security Fundamentals

Firewalls: Implementing firewalls to filter and monitor network traffic for security purposes.

Virtual Private Network (VPN): Using VPNs to create secure connections over public networks.

Intrusion Detection Systems (IDS) and Intrusion Prevention Systems (IPS): Deploying IDS and IPS to detect and prevent network attacks.

13. Computer Security Threats and Countermeasures

Malware: Understanding different types of malware, such as viruses, worms, and ransomware, and using antivirus software for protection.

Phishing: Recognizing phishing attempts and adopting safe practices to prevent falling victim to scams.

Data Encryption: Using encryption techniques to protect sensitive data from unauthorized access.

14. Troubleshooting Process and Tools

Identification: Identifying the problem and gathering relevant information to understand the issue.

Analysis: Analyzing possible causes and narrowing down the root cause of the problem.

Resolution: Implementing solutions to fix the issue and verifying that the problem is resolved.

15. Troubleshooting Motherboard, RAM, CPU, and Power

Diagnosing motherboard-related issues and performing necessary repairs or replacements.

Troubleshooting RAM and CPU problems and resolving them.

Addressing power-related issues and ensuring proper power supply to the system.

16. Troubleshooting Hard Drives and RAID Arrays

Diagnosing hard drive issues and repairing or recovering data as necessary.

Troubleshooting RAID configurations and resolving array-related problems.

17. Troubleshooting Network Issues

Identifying and resolving common network connectivity problems.

Diagnosing and fixing issues related to network protocols, IP addresses, and DNS.

18. Troubleshooting Mobile OS

Addressing common mobile OS issues, including app crashes and system slowdowns.

Troubleshooting mobile device hardware and network connectivity problems.

19. Environmental Controls

Maintaining the appropriate temperature and humidity levels in data centers and computer rooms.

Implementing proper ventilation and cooling systems to prevent equipment overheating.

20. Safety Procedures and Policies

Adhering to safety protocols when working with computer systems and electrical equipment.

Complying with company policies and industry standards to ensure a safe working environment.

21. Communication and Professionalism

Demonstrating effective communication skills when interacting with colleagues and clients.

Practicing professionalism in the workplace, including time management and meeting deadlines.

10.2 Exam-Taking Strategies

Excellent! Let's delve into exam-taking strategies to help you approach your assessments with confidence and efficiency. Adopting effective strategies can optimize your performance and maximize your chances of success:

1. Read and Understand the Instructions:

Carefully read all exam instructions before starting. Pay attention to the format, time limits, and any specific guidelines provided by the instructor.

2. Skim Through the Entire Exam:

Quickly glance through the entire exam to get an overview of the questions and allocate your time accordingly. Identify easy questions that you can answer quickly.

3. Focus on Your Strong Areas First:

Start with questions related to topics you are confident about. This builds momentum and boosts your confidence for tackling more challenging questions later.

4. Time Management:

Divide the exam duration by the number of questions to allocate time for each item. Monitor your progress to ensure you stay on track.

5. Answer What You Know First:

Answer the questions you are sure about first. This ensures you collect easy marks quickly and gives you more time for challenging questions.

6. Skip Difficult Questions Initially:

If a question seems particularly challenging, skip it and move on. Return to it later if time allows or after completing other questions.

7. Read Each Question Carefully:

Take the time to read each question thoroughly, and ensure you understand what is being asked before answering.

8. Use Elimination Technique:

If you are unsure about an answer, eliminate obvious incorrect choices to narrow down options and improve your chances of guessing correctly.

9. Manage Time for Long Answers:

For longer answers or essays, allocate time for planning, outlining, and writing each response to ensure a comprehensive and organized answer.

10. Use Bullet Points and Keywords:

For short answer questions, use bullet points and keywords to convey your understanding concisely.

11. Review Your Answers:

If time permits, review your answers before submitting the exam. Check for errors or missed questions.

12. Stay Calm and Focused:

Keep a positive mindset and remain calm during the exam. Don't let stress hinder your performance.

13. Review Exam Format and Past Papers:

Familiarize yourself with the exam format and structure. Practice with past papers or sample exams to simulate real exam conditions.

14. Avoid Cramming:

Focus on understanding the material rather than memorizing it last minute. Cramming can lead to confusion during the exam.

15. Manage Test Anxiety:

Employ relaxation techniques like deep breathing to manage test anxiety. Trust in your preparation and abilities.

16. Double-Check Your Work:

If you have extra time at the end of the exam, use it to review your answers. Look for any mistakes or omissions.

17. Budget Time for Multiple-Choice Questions:

For multiple-choice questions, avoid spending too much time on a single item. If unsure, make an educated guess and move on.

18. Use Visual Aids and Diagrams:

If allowed, use visual aids and diagrams to enhance your answers, especially for complex concepts.

19. Pace Yourself:

Avoid getting stuck on challenging questions. If you find yourself spending too much time on one question, move on and return later if time permits.

20. Answer All Questions:

Don't leave any questions unanswered. Even if unsure, attempt to provide an answer as partial credit might be awarded.

21. Review Underlined or Bolded Terms:

Pay attention to any underlined or bolded terms in the questions as they may offer valuable clues.

22. Manage Anxiety During the Exam:

If you encounter a difficult question that makes you anxious, take a deep breath and move on to the next question. Returning to the challenging question later with a calmer mind can help.

23. Don't Overthink:

Sometimes, the first answer that comes to mind is the correct one. Avoid overthinking and second-guessing your initial instincts.

24. Maintain Focus on the Task:

Stay focused on the exam and avoid distractions. If possible, sit in a quiet area to minimize disruptions.

25. Bring Necessary Materials:

Ensure you have all required materials, such as pens, pencils, calculators, or permitted resources, ready before the exam.

26. Follow the Format of the Answer Sheet:

If using an answer sheet, make sure to fill it out accurately and according to the instructions.

27. Read All Choices in Multiple-Choice Questions:

Read all options before selecting an answer. Sometimes, the correct answer might be the last one you read.

28. Use Abbreviations Sparingly:

Avoid excessive use of abbreviations, especially if they are not widely recognized. Be clear in your responses.

29. Manage Nervousness:

It's normal to feel nervous before an exam, but don't let it overwhelm you. Use the nervous energy to stay alert and focused.

30. Believe in Yourself:

Have confidence in your abilities and preparation. A positive mindset can boost your performance.

10.3 Resources for Additional Study

Here are some additional study resources you can explore to enhance your understanding of the topics covered in this guide:

1. Online Tutorials and Courses:

Platforms like Coursera, Udemy, and edX offer a wide range of courses on computer systems, networking, hardware, operating systems, and more. Look for courses taught by reputable instructors and organizations.

2. Official Documentation and Manuals:

For specific hardware components, operating systems, and software, refer to official documentation and manuals provided by the manufacturers or developers. These resources offer in-depth technical information.

3. YouTube Videos and Channels:

YouTube is a valuable resource for video tutorials and explanations on various computer-related topics. Look for reputable channels with quality content.

4. Online Forums and Communities:

Participate in online forums and communities dedicated to computer systems, networking, and troubleshooting. Ask questions, share knowledge, and learn from experienced individuals.

5. Practice Labs and Simulations:

Look for virtual labs and simulations that allow you to practice hands-on tasks related to hardware, networking, and operating systems without the need for physical equipment.

6. Online Articles and Blogs:

Many technology websites and blogs publish articles on computer-related topics. Search for authoritative sources to expand your knowledge.

7. Textbooks and E-books:

Refer to textbooks on computer systems, networking, hardware, and other relevant subjects. Many e-books are also available for easy access.

8. Tech Conferences and Webinars:

Attend technology conferences and webinars to gain insights into the latest trends and developments in the field.

9. Official Certification Study Materials:

If you are preparing for specific certifications (e.g., CompTIA A+, CCNA, etc.), use official study materials and practice exams offered by certification providers.

10. Educational Websites and Portals:

Websites like Khan Academy, TechRepublic, HowStuffWorks, and Techopedia offer educational content on various technology topics.

11. Online Courses from Universities:

Many universities offer online courses on computer science and related subjects. Check university websites for course offerings.

12. Academic Journals and Research Papers:

If you want in-depth knowledge on specific topics, explore academic journals and research papers related to computer systems, networking, and other subjects.

13. Online Tech Blogs and Podcasts:

Follow reputable tech blogs and podcasts that cover topics related to computer systems, networking, hardware, and software. They often provide valuable insights, industry news, and expert opinions.

14. Online Coding Platforms:

If you're interested in programming and software development, explore coding platforms like GitHub, Codecademy, and LeetCode to practice coding exercises and challenges.

15. Virtual Labs and Sandbox Environments:

Some websites and platforms offer virtual labs and sandbox environments where you can experiment with different operating systems, network configurations, and software setups in a safe and controlled environment.

16. Online Technology Magazines:

Subscribe to reputable technology magazines that regularly publish articles on a wide range of tech topics. Magazines like PCMag, Wired, and CIO provide insightful content.

17. Webinars and Webcasts:

Participate in webinars and webcasts organized by industry experts and technology companies. These sessions often offer valuable insights and demonstrations.

18. Official Vendor Documentation:

For certifications or specific hardware/software, explore official documentation provided by vendors like Cisco, Microsoft, Apple, and others.

19. Online Study Groups:

Join online study groups or forums dedicated to specific technology subjects. Collaborate with other learners to share knowledge and discuss challenging topics.

20. Networking Events and Meetups:

Attend local or virtual networking events and meetups related to technology and computer systems. Networking can lead to valuable connections and opportunities for learning.

21. Whitepapers and Case Studies:

Look for whitepapers and case studies from reputable companies and organizations. They often provide real-world scenarios and practical applications.

22. Technology YouTube Channels:

Subscribe to YouTube channels that focus on technology and computer-related content. Many channels offer tutorials, reviews, and demonstrations.

23. Online Practice Tests:

Use online practice tests and quizzes to assess your knowledge and identify areas for improvement. Some platforms offer timed mock exams to simulate real exam conditions.

24. Technology Podcasts:

Listen to technology podcasts hosted by industry experts and enthusiasts. Podcasts can be a great way to stay updated with the latest trends and discussions.

25. Online Learning Platforms from Universities:

Universities and colleges often offer online learning platforms that provide free or paid courses on computer-related subjects.

Quiz

1. What is the primary function of the Central Processing Unit (CPU)?
   a. Manage network connections
   b. Store data permanently
   c. Execute instructions and perform calculations
   d. Provide power to the computer

2. What type of memory is volatile and temporary, used to store data that the CPU needs to access quickly?
   a. Hard Disk Drive (HDD)
   b. Solid State Drive (SSD)
   c. Random Access Memory (RAM)
   d. Read-Only Memory (ROM)

3. Which component is responsible for providing communication between various hardware components in a computer system?
   a. Graphics Processing Unit (GPU)
   b. Power Supply Unit (PSU)
   c. Motherboard
   d. CPU

4. What does the acronym LAN stand for in networking?
   a. Local Access Network
   b. Long Area Network
   c. Local Area Network
   d. Limited Access Network

5. Which network device is used to connect multiple computers within a LAN and directs data packets to their destination?
   a. Router
   b. Modem
   c. Hub
   d. Switch

6. Which networking protocol is commonly used for accessing websites over the internet?
   a. TCP/IP
   b. FTP
   c. UDP

d. HTTP

7. Which type of mobile device operating system is developed by Google?

   a. iOS

   b. Android

   c. Windows Phone

   d. Blackberry OS

8. What does CPU stand for in the context of mobile devices?

   a. Central Processing Unit

   b. Cellular Phone Unit

   c. Compact Processing Unit

   d. Central Phone Unit

9. Which mobile network technology provides higher data speeds compared to 3G?

   a. 2G

   b. 4G

   c. 3G

   d. 5G

10. What is the first step in the troubleshooting process?

    a. Identify the problem

    b. Implement the solution

    c. Test the solution

    d. Gather information

11. What type of computer security threat is designed to spread from one computer to another and replicate itself?

    a. Phishing

    b. Ransomware

    c. Worm

    d. Trojan

12. Which computer security measure uses unique physical characteristics of individuals to grant access to a system?

    a. Password

    b. PIN

    c. Biometric authentication

    d. Two-factor authentication

13. Which component of a computer is responsible for long-term storage of data, even when the power is turned off?

    a. RAM

    b. CPU

    c. Hard Disk Drive (HDD)

    d. Power Supply Unit (PSU)

14. Which networking device operates at the Data Link Layer (Layer 2) of the OSI model and forwards data packets based on MAC addresses?

    a. Router

    b. Switch

    c. Hub

    d. Modem

15. Which mobile operating system is exclusive to Apple devices?

    a. Android

    b. Windows Phone

    c. iOS

    d. Blackberry OS

16. What is the process of converting data into an unreadable form to prevent unauthorized access?

    a. Hacking

    b. Encryption

    c. Phishing

    d. Decryption

17. Which type of troubleshooting focuses on identifying and resolving issues related to the computer's hardware components?

    a. Software troubleshooting

    b. Network troubleshooting

    c. Hardware troubleshooting

    d. Operating system troubleshooting

18. What is the purpose of a UPS (Uninterruptible Power Supply) in a computer system?

    a. Connect to the internet

    b. Provide backup power during outages

    c. Store data permanently

d. Manage network connections

19. Which network device operates at the Network Layer (Layer 3) of the OSI model and forwards data packets based on IP addresses?

    a. Router

    b. Switch

    c. Hub

    d. Modem

20. What is the default protocol used for sending emails over the internet?

    a. HTTP

    b. FTP

    c. SMTP

    d. POP3

21. What type of malware is specifically designed to lock users out of their own systems or files until a ransom is paid?

    a. Virus

    b. Worm

    c. Ransomware

    d. Trojan

22. Which component of a computer system converts AC power from the wall outlet into DC power used by the internal components?

    a. CPU

    b. PSU

    c. RAM

    d. GPU

23. Which network topology uses a central hub to connect all devices in the network?

    a. Star

    b. Ring

    c. Bus

    d. Mesh

24. Which mobile network technology provides the slowest data speeds and is primarily used for voice calls and text messaging?

    a. 4G

    b. 5G

c. 3G

d. 2G

25. Which technology is used to protect sensitive data, such as passwords and credit card numbers, during transmission over the internet?

a. Encryption

b. Decryption

c. Authentication

d. Authorization

26. Which mobile device feature allows users to determine their geographical location using GPS technology?

a. NFC (Near Field Communication)

b. Bluetooth

c. Wi-Fi

d. Location services

27. What does the acronym RAID stand for in the context of data storage?

a. Random Array of Independent Disks

b. Redundant Array of Independent Disks

c. Read Accessible Independent Disks

d. Rapid Array of Independent Drives

28. What is the purpose of a firewall in network security?

a. Protect data from physical theft

b. Prevent unauthorized access to a network

c. Encrypt data transmitted over the internet

d. Provide power backup during outages

29. Which type of software allows users to interact with the computer and run applications?

a. Operating System

b. Antivirus Software

c. Firmware

d. Device Driver

30. What is the primary role of a modem in networking?

a. Connect multiple devices within a LAN

b. Direct data packets to their destination

c. Encrypt data transmitted over the internet

d. Provide power backup during outages e. Establish a connection to the internet

Appendix: Answers to End-of-Chapter Quizzes

Chapter 1

1. Central Processing Unit
2. HTML
3. 1111
4. Random Access Memory (RAM)
5. b) macOS
6. Graphical User Interface
7. Internet of Things
8. Monitor
9. b) C
10. Intel Corporation
11. HyperText Markup Language
12. Local Area Network
13. Word processing software
14. Compiling
15. RAM (Random Access Memory)
16. Uniform Resource Locator
17. Operating system
18. Solid State Drive
19. JavaScript
20. Bus topology
21. Virtual Private Network
22. Random Access Memory
23. R
24. Central Processing Unit
25. ROM (Read-Only Memory)
26. Google Chrome
27. Dropbox
28. Linux
29. Managing hardware resources
30. Hard Disk Drive (HDD)

Chapter 2

1. B) Execute instructions and perform calculations
2. C) Random Access Memory (RAM)
3. C) Motherboard
4. B) BIOS
5. C) Hard Disk Drive (HDD)
6. PCIe
7. Printer
8. Touchscreen
9. B) To enhance gaming and graphics performance on laptops
10. B) RAID 1
11. C) RAM
12. B) USB
13. B) Network Interface Card (NIC)
14. D) To provide backup power in case of a power outage
15. B) Solid State Drive (SSD)
16. C) GPU (Graphics Processing Unit)
17. Unified Extensible Firmware Interface
18. HDMI
19. Microphone
20. PCI
21. To scan barcodes for product identification
22. To combine multiple storage drives into a single logical unit
23. Optical Drive
24. PCI
25. To enhance gaming and graphics performance on laptops
26. B) ROM
27. C) Sound Card
28. To provide backup power in case of a power outage
29. B) USB
30. C) GPU (Graphics Processing Unit)

Chapter 3

1. b) Execution of instructions
2. b) ROM
3. Basic Input Output System
4. Hard Disk Drive
5. Forward data packets between networks
6. SSL/TLS
7. Domain name to IP address resolution (Correct)
8. Twisted pair cable
9. Local Area Network
10. Bluetooth
11. b) SMTP
12. 5 Gbps
13. c) 255.255.255.0
14. Linear (Correct)
15. Universal Resource Locator
16. HTTP
17. Private IP address
18. 80
19. Switch
20. WPA2
21. Prevent unauthorized access and protect against cyber threats
22. IGMP
23. Voice over Internet Protocol
24. DNS
25. 1 Gbps
26. Provide wireless connectivity and act as a central hub for wireless devices
27. SSH
28. Check the connectivity to a remote host
29. DHCP
30. SMTP

Chapter 4

1. C. Execute instructions and perform calculations
2. C. RAM (Random Access Memory)
3. HDD (Hard Disk Drive)
4. Initialize hardware and boot the operating system
5. C. SSD (Solid State Drive)
6. B. Keyboard
7. C. Printer
8. B. Provide internet access to multiple devices in a LAN
9. D. Ethernet
10. B. POP3
11. Wireless Local Area Network
12. NFC (Near Field Communication)
13. Android
14. iOS
15. Send outgoing emails from the client to the server
16. HTTP
17. Ensure secure communication between email client and server
18. Encrypted files (PGP, S/MIME)
19. 5G
20. Bluetooth
21. GPU
22. Initialize hardware and boot the operating system
23. ROM
24. LAN (Local Area Network)
25. USB
26. Star
27. B. Router
28. B. HTTP (Hypertext Transfer Protocol)
29. Wi-Fi
30. B. Smartphone

Chapter 5

1. b) CPU (Central Processing Unit)
2. Initialize hardware and start the operating system
3. HDD (Hard Disk Drive)
4. To display graphics and images on the screen
5. Storage Device (e.g., HDD or SSD)
6. USB (Universal Serial Bus)
7. Local Area Network
8. Switch
9. Star Topology
10. HTTPS (Hypertext Transfer Protocol Secure)
11. b) Identify the problem
12. Wireshark
13. Check and repair file system errors on the hard drive
14. ping
15. Check physical connections and power
16. ipconfig (Windows) / ifconfig (Linux, macOS)
17. Test the hypothesis
18. Network monitoring tools
19. Reliable Array of Independent Disks
20. RAID 5
21. Android (or iOS)
22. iOS
23. Application
24. Fingerprint Scanner
25. The fourth generation of mobile networks
26. The fourth generation of mobile networks
27. 5G
28. Updating
29. GPS (Global Positioning System)
30. Answer not provided (Assuming it's the continuation of the previous question set.)
31. SMTP (Simple Mail Transfer Protocol)
32. DNS (Domain Name System)

33. Wireshark

34. Check and repair file system errors on the hard drive

35. ping

36. Check physical connections and power

37. ipconfig (Windows) / ifconfig (Linux, macOS)

38. Android (or iOS)

39. iOS

40. Application

41. Fingerprint Scanner

42. The fourth generation of mobile networks

Chapter 6

1. All of the above

2. c) Linux

3. APT

4. To run multiple operating systems on a single machine

5. BitLocker

6. Handoff

7. XFCE

8. To manage software installations and updates

9. Hyper-V

10. Command-Line Interface

11. macOS

12. To fix security vulnerabilities and bugs

13. apt install

14. Ansible

15. To backup and restore data

16. To manage software installations and updates

17. Windows Defender

18. Fedora

19. iCloud

20. b) XFCE

21. To load the operating system kernel into memory

22. CentOS

23. To deliver security updates and patches

24. Time Machine

25. To provide a centralized location for software installation and updates

26. Kali Linux

27. Spotlight Search

28. Pacman

29. b) To revert the system to a previous state (restore point) in case of issues

30. b) apt remove

Chapter 7

1. c) Detecting and removing malicious software

2. Manipulating individuals to disclose sensitive information

3. VPN

4. Monitoring and controlling network traffic based on security rules

5. Ransomware

6. Denial-of-Service (DoS) attack

7. Including a mix of uppercase and lowercase letters, numbers, and special characters

8. Adding an extra layer of security by requiring multiple forms of authentication

9. Trusted individuals with authorized access causing security breaches

10. Controlling and monitoring devices' access to the network based on security policies

11. b) Manipulating individuals to reveal sensitive information or perform actions

12. Network segmentation

13. Securing data during transmission to prevent eavesdropping

14. Phishing attack

15. Firewall

16. Monitoring and alerting about suspicious or malicious activity on the network

17. Trojan

18. Secure Sockets Layer/Transport Layer Security

19. Safeguarding data stored on storage devices from unauthorized access

20. Man-in-the-Middle (MITM) attack

21. Delete the email without opening the attachment.

22. Access Control List (ACL)

23. Identifying weaknesses and potential security risks in the network

24. b) Advanced Persistent Threat (APT)

25. b) Multi-Factor Authentication (MFA)

26. Controlling and monitoring data movement to prevent data leakage

27. SQL injection attack

28. Principle of least privilege

29. Encryption

30. Educating employees about cybersecurity best practices

Chapter 8

1. Connect and communicate between components

2. Bit

3. ALU (Arithmetic Logic Unit)

4. SSD (Solid State Drive)

5. Basic Input Output System

6. SSD (Solid State Drive)

7. Keyboard

8. CPU (Central Processing Unit)

9. LAN (Local Area Network)

10. Switch

11. POP3 (Post Office Protocol version 3)

12. Bluetooth

13. CPU (Central Processing Unit)

14. iOS

15. Touch ID

16. B. Disk Cleanup

17. Android

Chapter 9

1. Execute instructions

2. Solid State Drive (SSD)

3. Hard Disk Drive (HDD)

4. Basic Input Output System

5. CPU

6. Star

7. b) SMTP

8. Ethernet

9. b) Dynamic Host Configuration Protocol

10. Bluetooth

11. b) iOS

12. To monitor network traffic and block unauthorized access

13. Trojan horse

14. b) Biometrics

15. c) Security cameras

16. b) Identify the problem

17. b) CPU (Central Processing Unit)

18. Redundant Array of Independent Disks

19. Ring

20. FTP (File Transfer Protocol)

21. b) Hard Disk Drive (HDD)

22. To control the computer's basic operations and perform hardware checks during startup

23. c) Keyboard

24. c) DNS (Domain Name System)

25. c) To protect the computer from power outages and provide backup power

26. Android

27. To send, receive, and manage email messages

28. To direct network traffic and forward data between different networks

29. Hacking

30. Antivirus

Chapter 10

1. c. Execute instructions and perform calculations

2. c. Random Access Memory (RAM)

3. c. Motherboard

4. c. Local Area Network

5. d. Switch

6. d. HTTP

7. b. Android

8. Central Processing Unit

9. 4G

10. Identify the problem

11. Worm

12. Biometric authentication

13. Hard Disk Drive (HDD)

14. Switch

15. iOS

16. b. Encryption

17. c. Hardware troubleshooting

18. b. Provide backup power during outages

19. Router

20. SMTP

21. Ransomware

22. b. PSU (Power Supply Unit)

23. Star

24. 2G

25. Encryption

26. d. Location services

27. Redundant Array of Independent Disks

28. Prevent unauthorized access to a network

29. Operating System

30. Establish a connection to the internet

Made in United States
North Haven, CT
15 September 2023

41586406R00122